The Bible's Big Story

Our Story

A visual roadmap for the biblical journey

Harry Wendt

CROSSWAYS INTERNATIONAL
Minneapolis, MN

The Bible's Big Story—Our Story
was developed and written by
Harry Wendt, Minneapolis, MN, USA

Illustrations by
Knarelle Beard, Adelaide, SA, Australia

The Bible text in this publication is from the New Revised Standard Version of the Bible, copyright 1989 by the Division of Christian Education of the National Council of Churches of Christ in the United States of America, and used by permission.

The Bible's Big Story—Our Story
is published and distributed by
CROSSWAYS INTERNATIONAL
7930 Computer Avenue South
Minneapolis, MN 55435

ISBN 1-891245-14-7

Second Edition
10 9 8 7 6 5 4 3 2

Foreword

Some years ago, the New Tribes Mission sent Trevor McIlwain to the Philippines to work among the Palawano people on Palawan Island. The New Tribes Mission was born with a passion for reaching people with a "simple Gospel" that required little or no training to communicate.

Soon after McIlwain began serving the Palawano people, he tried teaching them some very basic biblical doctrines, such as "Five Things You Need to Know in Order to be Saved." He got nowhere. Then he tried working the people through John's Gospel, verse by verse. Once again, his teaching made little or no sense to his audience. McIlwain then realized that both methods failed because the people had never been taught the basic Old Testament narrative as one complete story, as a sequence of events. So he changed his approach.

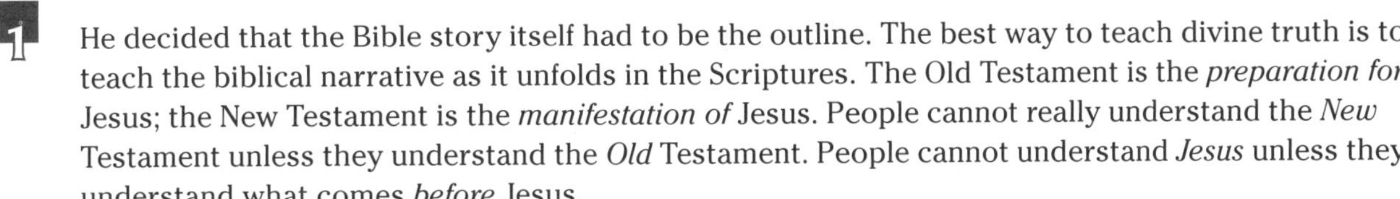

1. He decided that the Bible story itself had to be the outline. The best way to teach divine truth is to teach the biblical narrative as it unfolds in the Scriptures. The Old Testament is the *preparation for* Jesus; the New Testament is the *manifestation of* Jesus. People cannot really understand the *New* Testament unless they understand the *Old* Testament. People cannot understand *Jesus* unless they understand what comes *before* Jesus.
2. Other teaching methods should be used only when teaching people who have a clear panoramic view of God's dealings with humanity. In other words: Teach the *narrative* before you teach the *themes*.
3. We can learn what to emphasize from the Old Testament on the basis of what the Holy Spirit teaches and emphasizes in the New Testament. To put it another way: If you ignore the Old Testament, you ignore the source of the themes Jesus grapples with. At the same time, you must be alert to the manner in which Jesus *reinterprets* and *redefines* Old Testament themes. Jesus is the *final interpreter* of all Scripture. More, Jesus Himself is the final Word of God. In Jesus, truth becomes incarnate, truth becomes a Person.

Another missionary with important insights to share is Hans Rudi Weber. Weber was sent to Indonesia in 1952 by the Reformed Church to work among 30,000 nominal Christians. He was given no money and no co-workers. His helpers were to be the people he was sent to serve—people who had an average of three years of elementary education. Weber worked very successfully among his people, and eventually drew up some fundamental principles for communicating the Christian message. He emphasized the following:

1. It is a mistake merely to tell Bible stories. All must be set in the complete sweep of the biblical narrative from creation to the end-time, with Jesus at the center.
2. It is fundamentally wrong to translate and/or teach only the New Testament or New Testament portions. Jesus the Messiah must not be *de-Judaized* lest He be *de-historicized*. Otherwise, Christianity runs the risk of being placed in the same category as popular myths.

What do the conclusions reached by McIlwain and Weber say to us today? If we wish to make sense out of the New Testament, if we wish to understand Jesus, we must understand the storyline of the Old Testament as a whole. Note: the storyline *as a whole*—not just *fragments* of it, a piece here and a piece there. We must not treat the Bible as a collection of stories about a succession of so-called heroes to be selected at random—depending on the moral point of the moment. No! We must understand the storyline as a sequence of events through which is woven a series of key biblical themes. Then, when we reach the New Testament, we must ask, "How does Jesus handle the storyline? How does Jesus reinterpret and redefine its themes?" When we work that way, the Bible makes tremendous sense and challenges us enormously.

The time-line that this booklet explains has been produced to help people put the Bible's *little stories* together in such a way that they can see the Bible's *big story*.

Harry Wendt
Minneapolis, MN

Contents

A copy of Crossways International's *Biblical Tell-Tale Time-Line* is contained in the pocket inside the front cover of this book.

The Time-Line Codes

Take out the time-line from the pocket in the front cover of this book.

The time-line tells the story of Abraham and his descendants: the Israelites and the Jews. It culminates in presenting truths about the person and ministry of Jesus the Messiah.

The narrative that unfolds in the Bible is told from a theological and spiritual viewpoint. In many respects, it reads as a dialogue between God and His people, rather than as a diary that merely lists events.

Pages 3–6 contain tips for deciphering the symbols used in the time-line. The section which follows guides readers through the narrative and themes depicted in the time-line.

The two most obvious components of the time-line are:

- A set of ***22 numbered illustrations*** that depict key events and themes in the biblical narrative, with explanations beneath each frame.
- Periods of time, from ***1900*** B.C. to ***100*** A.D., indicated on ***large black circles***.

Immediately above the 22 frames (*beginning above frame 2*) is a ***horizontal, colored center line***, on and above which are ***figures***, ***illustrations***, ***numbers***, and ***symbols***. On the *upper right section* of the time-line are ***horizontal colored lines*** representing the histories of other nations and empires. ***Additional numbers*** are located on these lines. ***All numbers*** correspond to the ***numbered names of persons*** in the *top left section* of the time-line.

The numbers make use of a style-code.

1–14 a. ***First numbers*** *in the center line:* the judges, Joshua–Samuel.

b. ***White numbers in black boxes:*** kings of the united Israel (1–3), followed by kings of the Southern Kingdom of Judah (4–23).

c. ***Black numbers in white boxes:*** kings of the Northern Kingdom of Israel.

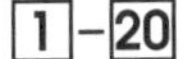

d. ***Yellow numbers in black boxes: MACCABEES & HASMONEANS*** (1–10); ***Herod the Great*** (11); ***Pontius Pilate*** (12). The Jewish people revolted against the Seleucids in 165 B.C., gained full independence in 142 B.C., but came under Roman control in ***63*** B.C.

e. ***Black numbers in white circles on scrolls:*** the Latter ***PROPHETS*** of Israel and Judah. The names of some of the postexilic prophets are not included: Joel, Obadiah, Jonah, Haggai, and Zechariah. The number "**3**" is placed on three scrolls—all of which are linked to the prophet ***Isaiah***. Some believe that, although Isaiah is responsible for all the writings that bear his name, chs. 1–39 deal with the period 742–701 B.C., chs. 40–55 speak to the Judeans in exile in Babylon, and chs. 56–66 relate to the Jews who were trying to reestablish the nation in Judah after they returned from Babylon. Others believe that the latter two sections were written by disciples from a "school of Isaiah" who perpetuated their master's work. The names ***ELIJAH*** and ***ELISHA*** appear between ***900*** and ***800*** B.C.; neither prophet left anything in writing.

f. ***Black numbers in yellow boxes*** *within the series of colored lines across the upper right section* of the time-line: Rulers who played a role in the history of Israel and Judah from the empires of ***ASSYRIA***, ***BABYLONIA***, ***PERSIA***, ***MACEDONIA/GREECE***, the Greek ***PTOLEMIES*** who ruled Egypt, the Greek ***SELEUCIDS*** who ruled Syria, and ***ROME***.

Immediately before the indicator for ***1900*** B.C. is a ***small black line***, ***clock face***, and ***question mark***—to indicate that the length of the time-span from creation to Abraham is not known.

The Time-Line Codes (continued)

 5

The ***three figures** in the center line to the right of **1900*** are ***ABRAHAM***, Sarah, and Isaac.

The ***four figures*** on the ***purple arrow** to the right of **1800*** are Isaac, Rebekah, Jacob, and Esau.

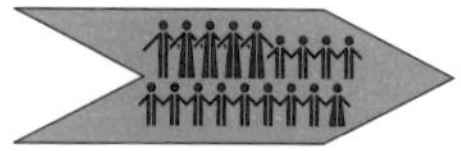

The next ***eighteen figures*** on the ***blue arrow*** are Jacob, his two wives, two concubines, twelve sons, and one daughter.

Following are an ***indefinite number of figures*** on the ***green arrow*** that represent the expanding Jacob clan.

The section in the center line consisting of ***black arrows*** on a ***yellow background*** denotes the period of time Jacob and his descendants lived in Egypt prior to the Exodus under Moses.

6

*To the left of the marker for **1600*** is a symbol for an ***Egyptian pyramid***, and a ***red arrow***. These symbols serve as reminders of Jacob and his extended family settling in Egypt at the time of Joseph.

7

The ***symbol for covenant*** appears in *frames 6, 11, and 14, and above frame 8*. The ***five black dots and the set of red law-code tablets*** represent the six parts of the covenant God made with the Israelites at Mt. Sinai.

8

Between the markers for ***1300*** and ***1200*** is a ***shattered Egyptian pyramid*** and a simplified depiction of the ***Exodus from Egypt*** (see frame 6). Some interpreters believe that the Exodus took place about 1450 B.C., two hundred years earlier than the date suggested on the time-line.

9

*Within the center line, between **1020** and **922*** B.C. (approximately), are numbers denoting the names of ***Saul*** ([1]), ***David*** ([2]), and ***Solomon*** ([3])—kings who ruled a *United Kingdom*. The ***red vertical jagged line at 922*** indicates that the United Kingdom split—into the *Northern Kingdom* of ***ISRAEL*** and the *Southern Kingdom* of ***JUDAH***. It is not known precisely how long Saul's son, ***Ishbosheth*** ([1]), ruled the Northern Kingdom after his father's death—possibly ***2–7 years***; see 2 Samuel 2:10; 5:5.

10

The horizontal line depicting northern kings contains ***blue, white, and magenta segments***; those in white are very narrow. The changing colors indicate the succession of the nine dynasties which ruled in Israel. The history of the Northern Kingdom came to an end when the Assyrians destroyed the realm in ***721*** B.C., 2 Kings 17.

11

Above seven of the numbered sections denoting the names of northern kings is a ***dagger***. The dagger indicates that the king listed beneath it was assassinated by his successor. Furthermore, ***Zimri*** ([6]) committed suicide after only seven days on the throne.

12

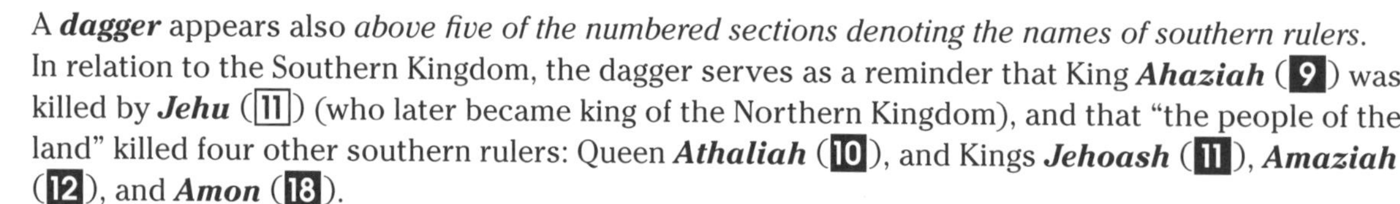

A ***dagger*** appears also *above five of the numbered sections denoting the names of southern rulers*. In relation to the Southern Kingdom, the dagger serves as a reminder that King ***Ahaziah*** ([9]) was killed by ***Jehu*** ([11]) (who later became king of the Northern Kingdom), and that "the people of the land" killed four other southern rulers: Queen ***Athaliah*** ([10]), and Kings ***Jehoash*** ([11]), ***Amaziah*** ([12]), and ***Amon*** ([18]).

The Time-Line Codes (continued)

13 *Just to the left of the marker for **700*** B.C. is a stylized symbol of Assyrian domination: an ***Assyrian king*** and a ***circle of chains***. The Assyrians under ***Sargon II*** (13) destroyed the Northern Kingdom in ***721*** B.C., and led thousands of its citizens into exile.

14 *To the right of the marker for **600*** is a symbol of Babylonian domination: a ***Babylonian ziggurat*** and ***circle of chains***. (A ziggurat was a pyramid-like structure with a temple on its summit.) ***Nebuchadnezzar*** (18) finally destroyed Judah, Jerusalem, and the Temple in ***587*** B.C. He took two kings into exile: ***Jehoiachin*** (22) in ***597*** B.C., and ***Zedekiah*** (23) in ***587*** B.C. Jehoiachin was still alive in 560 B.C., and 55 years of age, 2 Kings 25:27–30. Although many hoped that Jehoiachin would live through the exile and return to Jerusalem to reestablish the nation and the Davidic dynasty, he died in Babylon.

15 *To the right of the marker for **200*** B.C. is an illustration consisting of a ***sword***, the ***Jerusalem skyline***, a ***scroll***, and the ***Star of David*** (symbol for Judaism) It serves as a reminder that, during the period ***168–165*** B.C., Antiochus IV "Epiphanes" of Syria persecuted the Jewish people. Although he was willing to permit the Jews to live in Judah, he wanted to do away with Judaism and force the Jews to embrace Hellenism—Greek religious ideas and the Greek way of life. Antiochus desecrated the Jerusalem Temple and insisted that every Jew should eat a small portion of pork each year. He forbade the Jews to use their scriptures, to practice circumcision, to observe Jewish festivals and the Sabbath, etc. He also demanded that all his subjects acknowledge him as divine. Through the efforts of the ***MACCABEES*** (whose descendants were the ***HASMONEANS***), in 165 B.C. Antiochus' forces were driven from Jerusalem, the Temple was cleansed and rededicated, and Judaism was reestablished. The Pharisees (initially known as the *Hasidim*) and the Sadducees appear on the scene about this time.

After the death of ***Judas Maccabeus*** (1) in a battle in ***160*** B.C., his brother ***Jonathan*** (2) succeeded him—and gained for himself the office of High Priest (note the ***priest's headdress*** in the center line above frame 17). Jonathan was succeeded by his brother, ***Simon*** (3), under whom—in 142 B.C.—the Jewish people gained full independence from the ***SELEUCIDS*** (***Star of David***—symbol of the Jewish nation). Simon served as both High Priest and king (***crown***). The union of these two roles infuriated many Jewish people. Although the Maccabees were Levites, they were not descended from Zadok, David's priest—and they were not descendants of David.

Across the upper right section of the time-line are reminders of the spans of time during which neighboring powers were politically involved in the events outlined in the biblical narrative. The nations depicted are:

ASSYRIA

BABYLONIA

PERSIA

GREECE/MACEDONIA

PTOLEMIES

SELEUCIDS

ROME

Symbols for these various neighboring powers are also on the center line above the illustrations.

18 *Above the center line, and beneath the list of nations across the top*, are some ***small magenta dots and dashes***, ***names***, and ***dates***. They point to key persons and events within the sweep of biblical history, although some are not alluded to in the biblical text itself. They include the following:

a. *Above the circles bearing the numbers* ***500***, ***400***, and ***300*** are five names: ***BUDDHA***, ***CONFUCIUS***, ***SOCRATES***, ***PLATO***, and ***ARISTOTLE***. The first two are remote from the biblical narrative. The latter three were key figures in Greek history. Although they are not mentioned in the biblical narrative, they played an important role in formulating Greek thinking and religious ideas. Old and New Testament religious leaders had to respond to their teachings.

b. The Samaritans built a temple on Mt. Gerizim some time after 332 B.C.; the Hasmoneans destroyed it in ***128*** B.C.

c. The Romans under ***Pompey*** invaded Judah in ***63*** B.C. In ***19*** B.C., ***Herod*** the Great demolished the postexilic Temple and began constructing the magnificent edifice that is still referred to as "Herod's Temple." It took 82 years to build, and was completed in A.D. 63. About A.D. ***66***, the Jews revolted against Rome. In A.D. ***70***, the Romans crushed the revolt, and pushed Herod's Temple off its platform into the valleys to the east and south of the building.

d. In A.D. ***64–68***, ***Nero*** unleashed a persecution against the Christians, although on this occasion it was confined to Rome.

e. In A.D. ***95***, ***Domitian*** unleashed a persecution that spread more widely across the Roman Empire.

f. The Jews revolted against Rome once again in A.D. ***132*** under the leadership of ***Bar Kochba***, who was supported by Rabbi Akiba. This revolt was also put down and the Jews were now forbidden to live in Jerusalem.

Enter Jesus!

Finally, there came the day when the message of Jesus the Messiah and the Kingdom of God exploded out of Judea and began to spread around the Mediterranean world.

1 **Frame 19** contains symbols of Jesus' ***birth***, ***servant life***, ***crucifixion***, ***burial*** and ***return to life***, and His continuing presence.

2 **Frame 20** depicts Jesus the Messiah in the posture of a ***servant***, with a ***towel*** on His arm, and a ***basin*** of water before Him. Around Jesus is a circle of ***male and female figures holding hands in community***. Above Jesus is a ***dove***, the symbol for the Holy Spirit.

3 **Frame 21** shows a ***cross*** extending from the location of Jerusalem to that of Rome—to depict the message of Acts that eventually the Good News about Jesus' saving mission spread from the capital of the Jewish world to the capital of the Gentile world.

4 **Frame 22** contains numerous symbols which depict events the New Testament writers associate with the Final Day of history when Jesus the Messiah will reappear.

More detailed information about these final four frames is given in Part 2 of this book.

The Time-Line in Detail

As you read Part 2, please refer to the full-color time-line in the front pocket of this book. The individual frames are reproduced in the pages that follow.

The comments below expand on the notes printed on the time-line. Please read the notes beneath each corresponding frame on the fold-out color time-line first. Note that, on the reverse side of the time-line, there are additional explanations of some of the Bible's major themes.

Frames 1–3 need to be viewed as a whole, for they deal with the biblical prologue, Genesis 1–11. What does this imply? Although a Bible might contain, say, 1,500 pages of text, the call of Abraham is reported on perhaps page 15 in Genesis 12:1–3. Thus, one-percent of the biblical message leads up to the call of Abraham, and ninety-nine percent of it follows the call of Abraham.

In short: The first eleven chapters of Genesis reveal God's purpose in bringing creation and humanity into existence (Genesis 1:1–2:4a), and describe what went wrong, Genesis 2:4b–11:9. Genesis 11:10–32 describes Abraham's roots and origins. The enormous narrative that follows describes God at work in history to form a people for a mission: to draw all people back into fellowship with God and each other, in Jesus the Messiah, Ephesians 1:9,10.

Frame 1

Frame 1 is divided into ***five vertical segments***. In the *upper section* of ***segments* 2–5**, a ***yellow triangular section*** expands to the right, and a ***blue triangular section*** converges on, and points to, the ***three figures*** representing ***ABRAHAM***, Sarah, and Isaac (*above frame 2 on the time-line*). The arms of the ***indefinite number of figures*** in the expanding ***yellow triangular section*** are placed on the people's hips—to depict indifference to, and rebellion against, God. As the human race grew and chaos increased, God's focus of attention narrowed down until finally God called Abraham and Sarah, Genesis 12:1–3. God's plan was to use Abraham and Sarah to form a people through whom God would work to restore fallen creation and humanity (***frame 3***) to God's original intention (***frame 2***). God's plan of restoration was finally fully revealed and achieved in Jesus the Messiah (***frames 19–21***).

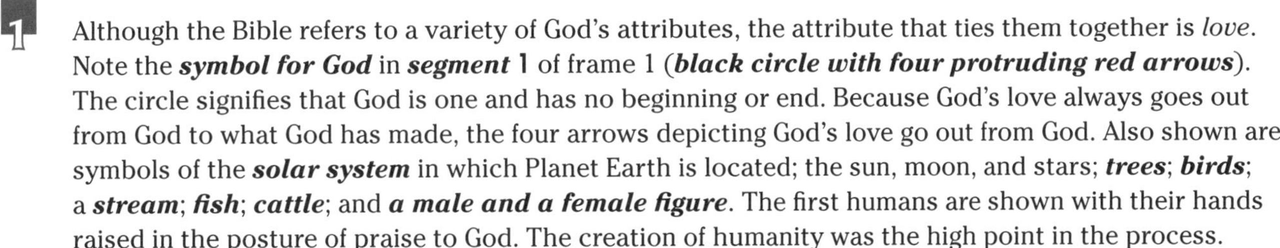

1 Although the Bible refers to a variety of God's attributes, the attribute that ties them together is *love*. Note the ***symbol for God*** in ***segment* 1** of frame 1 (***black circle with four protruding red arrows***). The circle signifies that God is one and has no beginning or end. Because God's love always goes out from God to what God has made, the four arrows depicting God's love go out from God. Also shown are symbols of the ***solar system*** in which Planet Earth is located; the sun, moon, and stars; ***trees***; ***birds***; a ***stream***; ***fish***; ***cattle***; and ***a male and a female figure***. The first humans are shown with their hands raised in the posture of praise to God. The creation of humanity was the high point in the process.

2 The *lower segments* of frame 1, ***segments* 2–5**, depict the events described in Genesis 2–11. The ***four curved red arrows*** (above the *upper segments* of frame 1) denote the ripple effect of the events shown in ***segments* 2–5** of the *lower section* of frame 1. We see the ripple effect of sin as it spreads outward from the ***first humans in the garden***, to ***their offspring in the fields***, to ***cosmic beings***, to the ***nations***. In ***segment* 2**, the relationship between ***God and humanity*** is broken (***fragmentation symbol***), as is that between ***male and female***. The ***green serpent*** between the ***man and woman*** reflects the narrative outlined in Genesis 3:1–7; read also Genesis 3:8–24.

Frame 1 (continued)

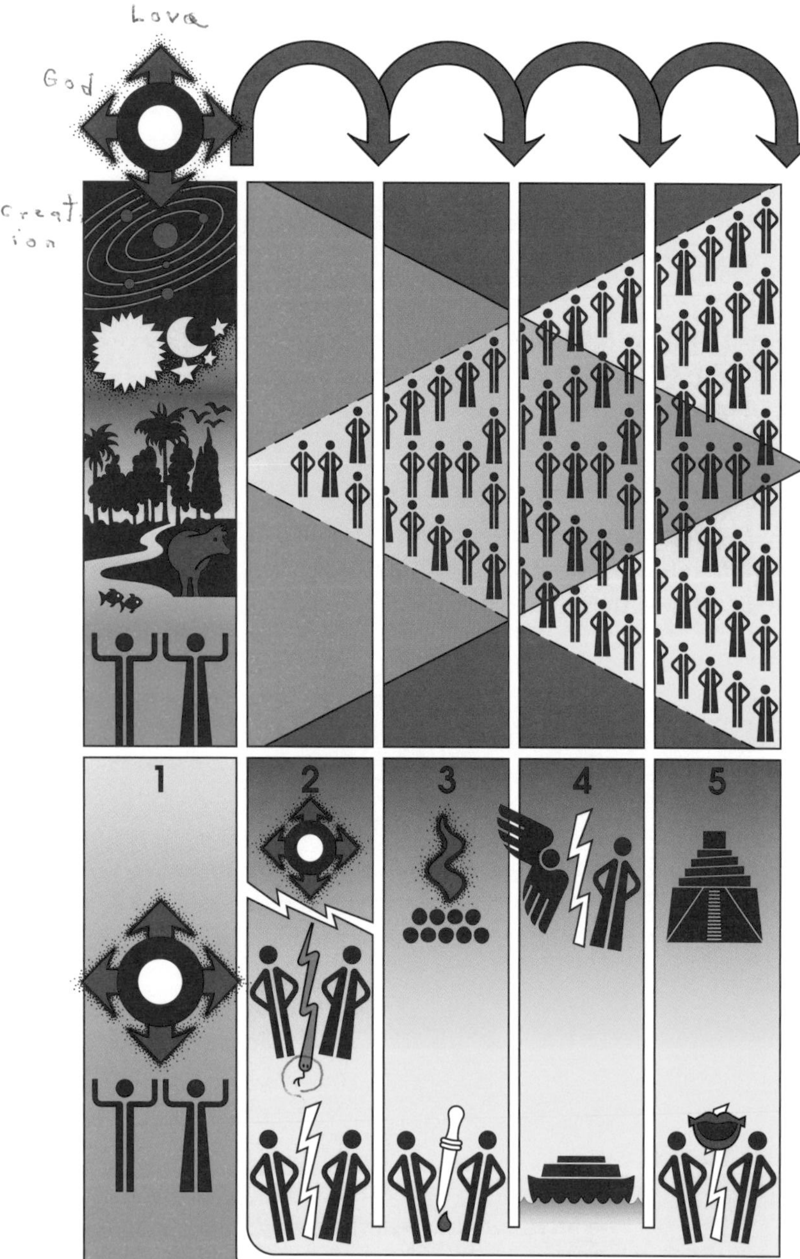

3 ***Segment* 3** refers to the relationship between ***brother and brother*** being broken. Cain and Abel (***two male figures***) offer sacrifices (***altar***) to God, Genesis 4:1–6. Abel's sacrifice is accepted; Cain's is not. Cain eventually kills Abel (***knife***, ***drop of blood***). The first murder gives rise to unbridled blood revenge, 4:17–26.

4 In ***segment* 4**, the ***heavenly and earthly*** realms are disrupted. According to some interpreters, Genesis 6:1–4 describes heavenly beings (***winged creature***), called "sons of God," being sexually intimate with earthly women (***female figure***). (For other references to "sons of God," see Job 1:6, 2:1, 38:7, Psalm 82:1.) In Genesis 6:5–9:29, God instructs Noah to build an ***ark***, through which God saves Noah and his family after sending a flood (***water***) to destroy the first creation. When the waters of the flood recede, a new beginning to creation takes place, and a new beginning to history and the human race gets under way through Noah, his family, and his descendants.

5 ***Segment* 5** depicts the fragmentation between ***nation and nation*** outlined in Genesis 11:1–9. People decide to build a ***tower*** that will reach up into the heavens—to make a name for themselves (i.e., to draw attention to themselves), and to avoid being scattered. God stops the project by introducing a variety of languages (***mouth***), and divides and scatters (***fragmentation symbol***) the different language groups across the face of the earth.

Frame 2

1 Frame 2 depicts God's original plan for humanity. God created the universe, ***Planet Earth***, and people to live on it. **God's plan was that people should live to serve God by serving each other in community.** Hence, superimposed on the world are ***two people in a kneeling, servant posture***. Around the world is a ***circle of male and female figures***, holding hands in ***community***. A ***blue line*** runs from the *bottom of frame 2 to the left*, and connects with ***segment* 1** of frame 1. The blue line illustrates the link between the wonders of God's creation and God's purpose in creating humanity.

2 In today's Western world, considerable emphasis is placed on the importance of the individual. The biblical materials focus on the concept of community. People are to see themselves as:

- Made and owned by God;
- Managers of a planet made and owned by God;
- Entrusted with powers of will, emotion, body, and intellect which they are to develop to glorify God and serve others—by helping others develop their powers of will, emotion, body, and intellect.

In all things, success is not to be measured in terms of the material goods people might acquire and enjoy. Success is to be measured only in terms of how much a person conforms to God's original plan for humanity, and helps others to do the same.

Frame 3

1 The *lower section* of frame 3 depicts the significance of the events in Genesis 2:4b–11:32. Sin breaks into the world (***shattered Planet Earth***, ***lightning flash***, ***symbol for sin*** superimposed) and destroys God's plan for humanity. Sin is shown as a ***red circular arrow***, signifying that people no longer serve God and others, but themselves. Inside five of the circular arrows are ***figures*** representing people.

The numbers in the *upper section* of frame 3 refer to the five major narratives contained in the first eleven chapters in Genesis that describe the severing of relationships (***fragmentation symbols***, ***knife***, ***drop of blood***, ***lips***) between:

1. ***God and humanity***, Genesis 3.
2. ***Male and female***, Genesis 3.
3. ***Brother and brother*** (Cain and Abel), Genesis 4,5.
4. The ***heavenly and earthly*** realms (cosmic chaos, perhaps), Genesis 6–9.
5. ***Nation and nation*** (the tower of Babel), Genesis 10,11.

2 Frame 3 and ***segments* 2–5** of frame 1 depict what went wrong with creation and humanity. A ***yellow line*** runs from *near the bottom of frame 3 to the left* to link it to ***segments* 2–5** of frame 1. Compare these sections with frame 2 and the ***segment* 1** of frame 1, both of which depict God's original plan.

Some of the key themes in the first eleven chapters of Genesis are:

a. Generation—Degeneration—Regeneration.

b. Formation—Disintegration—Restoration.

God made the universe and all within it to function harmoniously. It came apart. God is at work, through His people, to put it back together again. The great Swiss theologian, Karl Barth, once said, "The Church is formed to be a provisional display of God's original intention." The Anglican Catechism defines the mission of the Church by asking a question, and then answering it:

Question: *What is the mission of the Church?*

Answer: *The mission of the Church is to restore all people to unity with God and each other, in Christ.*

In Ephesians 1:9,10, Paul writes (RSV translation):

> *God has made known to us in all wisdom and insight the mystery of his will, according to his purpose which he set forth in Christ as a plan for the fullness of time, to unite all things in him, things in heaven and things on earth.*

To see how the time-line reflects these statements by Karl Barth and the Anglican Catechism, note first the original plan in frame 2, then note the chaos depicted in frame 3, and finally, in frames 19–22, see God's original intention restored in Jesus the Messiah. In Jesus' community, people are forgiven by grace, and restored to servant unity with God and each other.

Frame 4

2

Abraham

1 Genesis 12:1–3 describes God's initial call of Abraham. When God's good creation came apart, and chaos broke in among humanity at all levels, God called one man (***Abraham***) and one woman (***Sarah***), and declared that God would form a people (***three small figures***) out of them—through whom God would work to restore all people to unity with God and each other. Note the ***blue and purple arrow*** going from the *top left of frame 4 to the left* pointing to ***ABRAHAM*** and Sarah (*inside the* ***circle****, above frame 2 on the* ***center line***), and Isaac standing next to them.

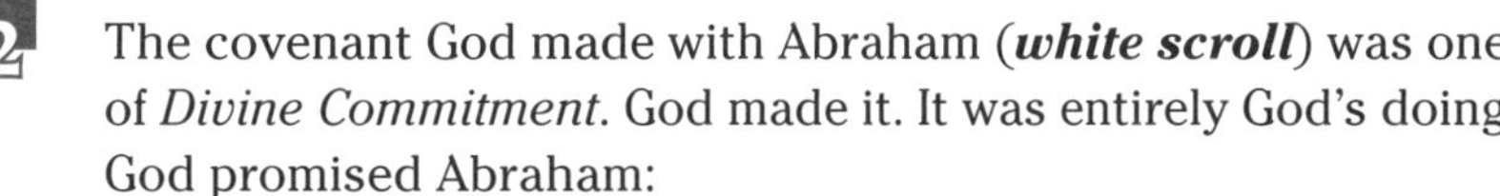

2 The covenant God made with Abraham (***white scroll***) was one of *Divine Commitment*. God made it. It was entirely God's doing. God promised Abraham:

a. Land (***Promised Land in yellow circle***);

b. Offspring (***extended family—male and female figures***);

c. The nations would be blessed through Abraham and his descendants. This aspect of God's covenant with the patriarchs is depicted by a ***cup of blessing*** placed above ***Israel***, but pouring its contents over the ***world***. Israel was not formed merely to enjoy material blessings, but to serve as a means through which God might bring divine blessings to the world—ultimately in the gift of Jesus the Messiah, the forgiving Savior and Servant Lord of humanity.

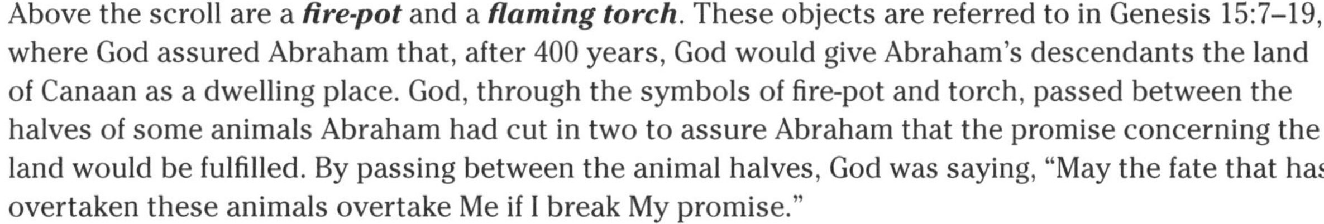

3 Above the scroll are a ***fire-pot*** and a ***flaming torch***. These objects are referred to in Genesis 15:7–19, where God assured Abraham that, after 400 years, God would give Abraham's descendants the land of Canaan as a dwelling place. God, through the symbols of fire-pot and torch, passed between the halves of some animals Abraham had cut in two to assure Abraham that the promise concerning the land would be fulfilled. By passing between the animal halves, God was saying, "May the fate that has overtaken these animals overtake Me if I break My promise."

The structure and spirit of this covenant are based on an ancient Royal Grant Treaty, examples of which have been unearthed by archaeologists during recent decades. In a treaty of this kind, a powerful benefactor bestowed a gift, such as land, on a much less powerful person or ruler. In spirit, it was a one-way affair.

Jeremiah 34:18-20

Frame 5

2

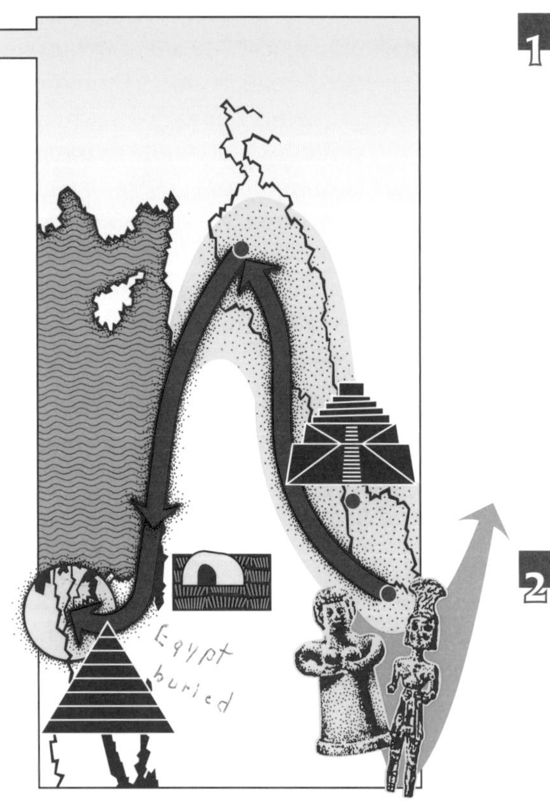

1 Frame 5 depicts events in the lives of the patriarchs: Terah, and his sons Abraham, Nahor, and Haran. Haran died in Ur of the Chaldees, Genesis 11:28. Terah and his clan eventually traveled northwest from Ur (location marked with ***red dot***, *lower right*), past Babylon (***red dot***, ***ziggurat***—sacred pyramid crowned with a temple) through the Fertile Crescent to Haran (***red dot***, *upper center*), where he and Abraham and their families eventually settled. (Haran was not only the name of one of Abraham's brothers; it was also the name of the location where the patriarchs settled.) Abraham's father, Terah, died in Haran. According to Genesis 11:31, God called Abraham while he was living at Haran. Abraham, Sarah, and Lot (Haran's son and Abraham's nephew) then traveled south to Canaan.

2 Genesis 12:10–20 describes how, because of a drought in Canaan, Abraham and his family went south to Egypt (***Nile Delta***, ***pyramid***, *lower left*) to have access to a sure supply of food and water. They eventually returned to Canaan to reside there. The Jacob and Joseph narratives describe how Abraham's descendants eventually moved back to Egypt and took up residence in the region of Goshen, Genesis 37–50.

3 The Genesis narrative describing the life of Abraham and Sarah contains a series of stories designed to keep readers in suspense: "Will Abraham be able to keep Sarah as his wife," 12:10–20; 20:1–18? "Will Abraham and Sarah ever have children," 15:1–5; ch. 16; ch. 21; ch. 22? "Will they ever gain possession of the land," ch. 13; 15:7–21; ch. 23? *The promises made in Genesis 12:1–3 are at stake throughout!*

4 Although God told Abraham that he and his descendants would receive the land of Canaan as a trust from God, at the close of his life all that Abraham owns of the Promised Land is a small ***field*** and a ***burial cave*** (*lower center*) which he bought from Ephron the Hittite for 400 shekels of silver, Genesis 23.

5 Scattered throughout the narrative are stories that describe the origins of those seven neighboring nations (note the reference to "seven," Mark 8:5,8) that eventually troubled and harassed Israel: Canaanites, 9:25; Ishmaelites, ch. 16; Ammonites and Moabites, 19:30–38; Midianites, 25:2; Edomites, 25:19–34; Amalekites, 36:12.

6 The Genesis narrative that follows focuses on several key themes:

a. How Jacob (Isaac's son) manages to outwit his brother, Esau, 25:23; 25:29–34; ch. 27;

b. How Jacob obtains wives and his twelve sons, chs. 28–35;

c. How and why the people God eventually called out of Egypt in the Exodus first settled in Egypt, chs. 37–50.

7 God did not call Abraham because of any goodness or virtue in Abraham. Joshua 24:2 states that when the Lord called the patriarchs, they were worshiping idols. Joshua 24:14,15 states that the descendants of the patriarchs were still worshiping idols in Egypt prior to the Exodus event; see also Ezekiel 20:1–9. Note the ***blue arrow*** linked to the ***idols*** in the *lower right of frame 5*, and pointing also to the Nile Delta of Egypt (***circle of chains***) in frame 6.

Frame 6

2

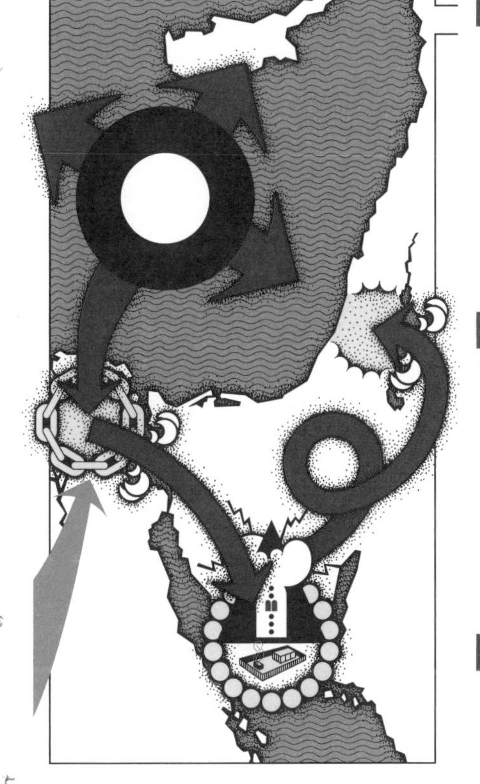

1 Frame 6 depicts the *key narrative* of the Old Testament—the Exodus from Egypt. At the close of the Genesis narrative, Jacob and his family are happily settled in Egypt. Several centuries later, at the beginning of the narrative in Exodus, their descendants are in bondage in that land (***circle of chains***). Why? There had come to power a pharaoh who no longer remembered the noble services that Joseph had rendered to previous pharaohs, and eventually enslaved the Israelites, Exodus 1:8.

2 God (***symbol for God***) intervened to rescue His people. He dealt with the pharaoh through a series of plagues, and then led the Israelites out of Egypt (***first red arrow***), opening up the waters (***white-capped waves***) in the process. God then guided the people to Mt. Sinai (***black triangle***) where He made a covenant with them (***white symbol*** resembling a door or a window), Exodus 1–20. A ***cloud*** and ***flashes of lightning***, symbolizing God's presence (Exodus 19:16–18), surround Mt. Sinai's summit.

3 God did not "come down" to the top of Sinai. Rather, the symbols of the divine presence which led Israel out of Egypt "appeared" at the top of Sinai, and later "descended" to rest above the Ark of the Covenant in the ***Tabernacle*** (depicted in yellow beneath Mt. Sinai). The Tabernacle, a portable shrine, was a way of making God's presence *transportable*. Furthermore, it was virtually a half-scale model of the structure King Solomon eventually built, perhaps to suggest to later generations that the Jerusalem Temple was so sacred, so important, that God had revealed its ground-plan to Moses at Mt. Sinai.

4 Note the ***five black dots*** and the ***red law-code tablets*** on the symbol for covenant in frames 6, 11, and 14; these represent the six chief parts of the covenant God made with Israel at Sinai. The structure of the Sinai Covenant reflects that of a six-part Suzerainty Treaty between a Hittite king and a vassal (subservient) ruler; see point 5 below. The third section of the Sinai covenant, consisting of stipulations or commandments, called the people to serve God and each other in community (***circle of yellow dots*** around Sinai).

5 It is incorrect to define the events at Sinai as the *giving of the commandments*. Rather, God *made a covenant* with Israel at Sinai. The opening section of Exodus 20 contains three major parts of this covenant formula.

1. **Preamble:** God begins by telling the people who God is: "I am the Lord your God."
2. **Historical Prologue:** Next, God tells the people what God has done for them: "Who brought you out of the land of Egypt, out of the house of bondage."
3. **Stipulations:** The third part of the covenant formula consists of the collection of laws traditionally called the Ten Commandments. Exodus, Leviticus, Numbers, and Deuteronomy contain additional collections of stipulations.

There are three more parts to the covenant formula, although they are not included in Exodus 20:

4. **Preservation and Rereading:** God tells the people to write out the covenant, to preserve it, and to teach it to all in Israel. See Joshua 24:25,26.

5. **Witnesses:** There are many witnesses to the covenant God has made with the people; the people must take it very seriously. See Joshua 24:27.
6. **Blessings and Curses:** If the people take the covenant seriously, things will go well with them; if they do not, things will go badly. See Deuteronomy 28.

6 The stipulations or commandments were not given to enable the Israelites to *affect* a relationship with God. Rather, they were intended to serve as guidelines to *reflect* a relationship with God. They were to serve as guidelines for:

- copying God;
- living in community;
- witnessing: to equip the Israelites to be a magnet to draw other people into God's family; see Deuteronomy 4:1–8;
- experiencing blessings: When people know God and do God's will, they experience inner joy and peace.

7 God then led the people (***second looped red arrow***) through the Sinai wilderness to a location on the East Bank of the Jordan River, just to the north of the Dead Sea, Numbers 10:11–Deuteronomy 1. There God opened up the waters once again (***white-capped waves***) to lead the people into the Promised Land of Canaan (***yellow starburst***), Joshua 3.

8 The covenant God made with Israel at Sinai was different from the one God made with Abraham. The covenant of *Divine Commitment* that God made with Abraham was entirely one of *promise*—one in which God stated what God would do for Abraham and his descendants *in the future*. The covenant made at Sinai was one of *Human Obligation*. In this latter covenant, God spelled out:

- Who God is.
- What God had done for the people *in the past*.
- The commandments—which were to serve as guidelines for *responding* to God's goodness.

9 Note the ***white and blue arrow*** going from the *top of frame 6* to the ***symbol for covenant*** *in the center line*. This points to the place in history where the events of the Exodus took place.

Frame 7

2

1 Frame 7 depicts the conquest of Canaan by the Israelites under Joshua—as outlined in the book bearing Joshua's name. It shows ***Joshua blowing on a shofar*** (ram's horn) to summon the people to battle. (Note the ***white and red arrow*** going from the *top of frame 7* to the number **1** representing Joshua's name *in the center line.*)

2 *In the center* of Frame 7 is the ***Ark of the Covenant*** and a ***sword***. God, whose divine presence is symbolized by the Ark of the Covenant, led (***magenta lines***) the people through the ***Jordan River*** and into the land. (The Jordan River is depicted by the ***dark line*** between the ***Sea of Galilee*** to the north, and the ***Dead Sea*** to the south.) Then, according to the book of Joshua, God led the people into battle against the Canaanites in a *Holy War*, symbolized by the sword.

3 Preparations for the conquest are described in Joshua 1–5. The conquest itself is outlined in Joshua 6–12. The manner in which the land was divided among the 12 tribes of Israel is explained in Joshua 13–21.

4 The ***phalanxes of magenta arrows*** denote Israel's capture of the Transjordan, and the southern and northern regions of Canaan. The ***white dots*** on the magenta lines point to the locations of cities referred to in the Joshua narrative.

5 Some of the key thoughts in the conquest narrative are:

a. God is the *Commander-in-chief* of Israel's armies.

b. Joshua is God's *general.*

c. The conquest is undertaken by a *united Israel.*

d. The conquest is *swift* and *complete*.

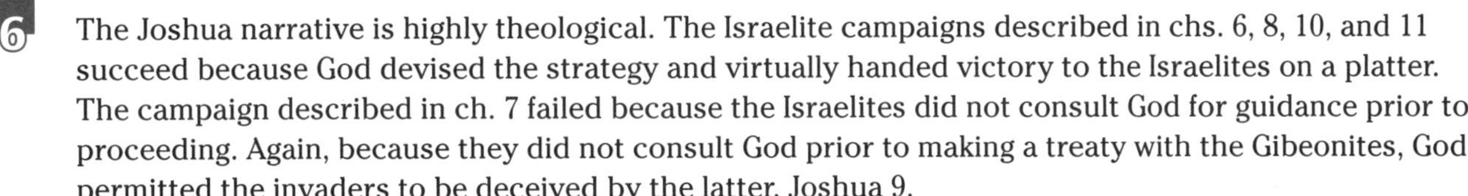

6 The Joshua narrative is highly theological. The Israelite campaigns described in chs. 6, 8, 10, and 11 succeed because God devised the strategy and virtually handed victory to the Israelites on a platter. The campaign described in ch. 7 failed because the Israelites did not consult God for guidance prior to proceeding. Again, because they did not consult God prior to making a treaty with the Gibeonites, God permitted the invaders to be deceived by the latter, Joshua 9.

Frame 8

2

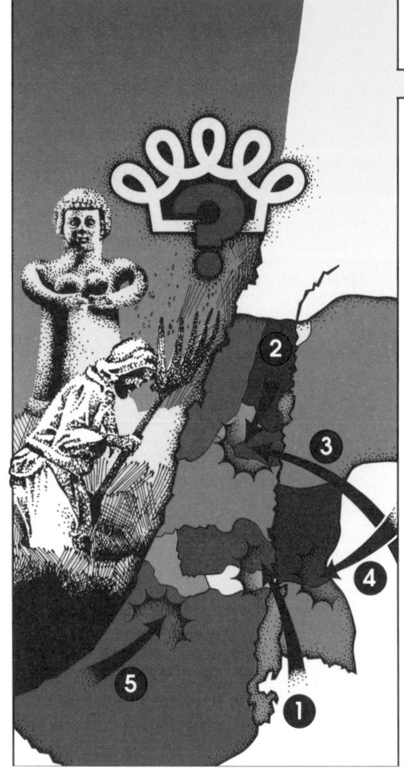

1 Frame 8 focuses on the period of the judges. The judges were military leaders, whom God raised up to govern and liberate God's people. Note the ***yellow and magenta arrow*** going from the *top right of frame 8 to the center line* on which are listed the numbers (**1–14**) representing names of the thirteen leaders referred to in the Book of Judges, plus that of Samuel. (The numbers correspond to those in the *list of judges on the top left of the time-line.*)

2 At the *left center* of frame 8 is a symbol of the fertility gods, or weather gods (***yellow idol***), that the Israelites worshiped after they entered the land of Canaan. The actual images were not as large as the illustration suggests. They were perhaps three to six inches high, either male or female in form, with accentuated sexual features. Beneath the image is a Canaanite ***farmer harvesting his crops***.

3 In Egypt, the Israelites relied upon the Nile River for their water supply. However, after the Israelites entered the land of Canaan, they found themselves having to farm under conditions very different from those that they had known in Egypt. Because they now had no access to a water source such as the Nile, irrigation was no longer possible. The Israelites, therefore, began to join the Canaanites in their worship rituals, some of which were sexual in nature, in the hope that the "local gods" would provide rain for their crops to ensure good harvests and a plentiful supply of food.

4 The cycle of events woven into each episode describing the activities of the successive judges is given in Judges 2:11–19:

- Israel sins by worshiping the Canaanite gods.
- God permits a neighboring nation to harass Israel.
- The Israelites cry to God for help.
- God raises up a judge to deliver His people.
- Once more, Israel sins—and the cycle is repeated.

5 Judges 1:1–2:10, among other things, contains a second report of Joshua's death; see Judges 2:8,9 and Joshua 24:29,30. The first two chapters of Judges create the impression that the various tribes tried to capture the land allotted to them on an *individual basis*, tribe by tribe (the twelve tribes of Israel were descended from, and named after, Jacob's twelve sons, Genesis 46:8–24). Hence, it is possible that the book of Joshua describes how Israel *should have* carried out the conquest, while the book of Judges reports *what actually happened*.

6 The book of Judges refers to thirteen judges from nine different tribes. The ***numbered arrows*** in frame 8 depict the five major campaigns described in its narrative:

❶ ***Ehud*** overthrows the Moabites, Judges 3:12–30.

❷ ***Deborah*** and Barak fight the Canaanites, Judges chs. 4,5.

❸ ***Gideon*** overcomes the Midianites and Amalekites, Judges 6–8.
❹ ***Jephthah*** defeats the Ammonites, Judges 10–12.
❺ ***Samson***, a Danite, battles the Philistines, Judges 13–16.

7 The Samson narrative actually extends to ch. 18; it was because of Samson's death that the Danites eventually decided to migrate north to Laish, chs. 17,18. They took with them a priest, a shrine, and some images from Ephraim (where nevertheless "God" and "the Lord" were worshiped; note 17:2,3,13 and 18:5,6), and used them to establish a shrine in their new territory.

8 Chs. 19–21 report how Benjaminites obtained wives from Jabesh-gilead—a gruesome tale from start to finish. There are several connections between this incident and Israel's first king, Saul, a Benjaminite. It is possible that Saul's mother or wife was among the women abducted from Jabesh-gilead to become wives for the Benjaminites. Saul's relatives most likely held positions of influence there. His first royal residence was at Gibeah, the setting for the incident that sparked the decimation of the tribe of Benjamin. Saul later rescued Jabesh-gilead from the Ammonites, 1 Samuel 11. They, in gratitude, rescued the bodies of Saul and his sons from where the Philistines had disposed of them, and dealt with them in an appropriate manner, 1 Samuel 31.

9 The events outlined in Judges reveal that, if Israel wished to survive in Canaan, the tribes would have to do three things:

- establish *national unity*.
- establish a system of government with *political continuity*.
- establish *spiritual purity*, and do away with polytheism.

10 ***Crown*** and ***question mark***: Kings: To be or not to be? That was the question! First and Second Samuel reveal how it was answered.

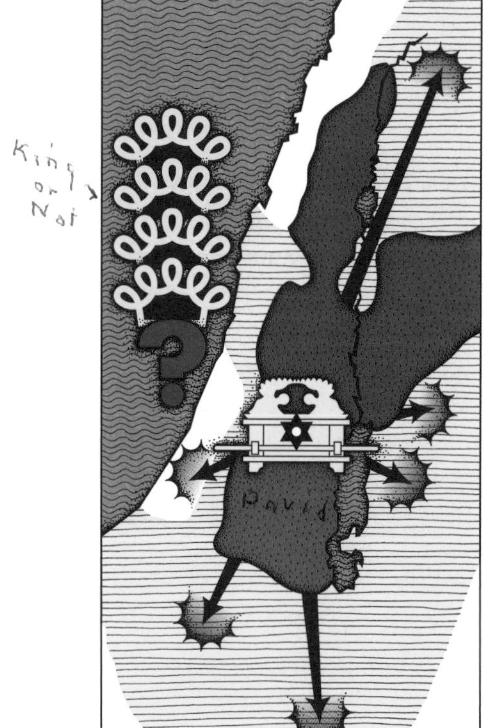

1 Israel had been led by judges and priests. But there were continuing problems with this leadership. The narratives that outline how Israel first came to have a king are complex, 1 Samuel 8–11. Some favor having a king; some oppose the move. Throughout the debate, two words are used to describe the coming ruler: king (in Hebrew, *melek*) and prince (in Hebrew, *nagid*). Wherever the narrative uses the term "prince," it views the appointment favorably. On the other hand, although the term "king" can be viewed favorably, whenever the coming appointment is viewed unfavorably, the term "king" is always used. Saul is viewed favorably in all of these four chapters.

To understand the Old Testament narrative, it is essential to be familiar with those detailed sections of Scripture which outline the reigns of Saul, David, Solomon, and Josiah. (See Parts 6 and 7.)

2 Eli's two sons were considered unfit to succeed their father as priests, 1 Samuel 2:22. Samuel's two sons were also looked on as unfit to follow in their father's footsteps, 1 Samuel 8:1–3. The cry for a king went up immediately after the events described in the latter passage.

3 The narrative outlined in Judges states that the spirit of God came upon the judges Othniel, 3:10; Gideon, 6:34; Jephthah, 11:29; and Samson, 13:25, 14:6,19, 15:14. The spirit of God also came upon Israel's first king, Saul (1 Samuel 10:10, 11:6,) and then upon King David, 1 Samuel 16:13. However, the spirit of God did not come upon any king after David—when succession was determined by primogeniture (the oldest son succeeded his father). However, the spirit of God then came on the prophets.

4 After Saul's death, David first gained control of the Southern Kingdom of Judah, 2 Samuel 2:1–4a. A period of two to seven years passed before David gained control of the Northern Kingdom of Israel, 2 Samuel 2:10, 5:5. (It is difficult to determine the exact length from the text.) After uniting the realm, David moved his capital from Hebron in central Judah to Jerusalem—on the border between Judah and Israel, 2 Samuel 5:6–10. He then brought the ***Ark of the Covenant*** to ***Jerusalem*** (*location marked by a star*), and placed it into a tent he had built to house it, 2 Samuel 6. Although he expressed a desire to build a Temple to house the Ark, God told him not to do so, and informed him that God would build a "house" out of David—a dynasty, 2 Samuel 7:1–17.

5 David greatly expanded his realm (***arrows*** pointing out from ***Judah***, *magenta area*, and ***Israel***, *red area*) by conquering and annexing the Syrians to the north, the Ammonites and Moabites to the east, the Edomites to the southeast, and the Amalekites to the southwest, 2 Samuel chs. 8, 10. Although he subdued the Philistines (to the west of Jerusalem), he did not incorporate them into his realm; apparently he employed Philistine soldiers as mercenaries to serve as his personal bodyguard, 2 Samuel 8:18, 15:18. The ***yellow region*** represents the territory David eventually conquered and subsumed into the kingdom of Israel.

6 ***Four crowns*** and ***question mark***: A fierce struggle to gain the throne took place among David's sons:

- Amnon raped his half-sister, Tamar, and was killed by her brother, Absalom, 2 Samuel 13.

Frame 9 (continued)

2

- Absalom revolted from his father and declared himself king in Hebron and then Jerusalem, but was eventually killed by his cousin, Joab, 2 Samuel 15–19.
- When David was well advanced in years, his son Adonijah declared himself to be king, and arranged for his own coronation, 1 Kings 1:1–10.
- Adonijah was eventually outsmarted by Nathan the prophet and David's wife Bathsheba (Solomon's mother)—who persuaded David to appoint Solomon as his successor, 1 Kings 1:11–2:12.

Frame 10

1 Frame 10 depicts key events in the reign of Solomon. Of the ten chapters 1 Kings devotes to the reign of Solomon, almost five chapters describe Solomon's building projects in Jerusalem, and most of these five chapters focus on the building and dedication of the ***Temple***.

2 Immediately after gaining the throne, Solomon killed his brother Adonijah, exiled the priest Abiathar who (like Joab) had supported the candidacy of Adonijah for the throne, killed Joab (David's nephew and general, and therefore Solomon's cousin) and a Benjaminite, Shimei, who had cursed David (2 Samuel 16:5–14) when he was fleeing from Absalom, 1 Kings 2:13–46.

3 The narrative describing Solomon's reign suggests that the Temple would stand forever (1 Kings 8:13), and that Jerusalem was the place God had chosen for God's name to dwell, 1 Kings 8:16; but note also Jeremiah 7:12, where the prophet states that Shiloh is the place where God made His "name to dwell at first."

4 The word "if" shows up frequently in the narrative that describes Solomon's reign, and makes virtually every previous promise conditional. *If* the king and people do not walk in the ways of David (i.e., worship one God in one Temple in one city, Jerusalem), they will lose their status as God's people, 1 Kings 6:11–13; the Davidic dynasty, 1 Kings 9:4,5; the land, 9:6,7; and the Temple, 9:8,9.

5 The conditional nature of God's promise was reiterated by the prophet Micah, writing about 200 years later, who stated in no uncertain terms that Jerusalem and the Temple would be destroyed. This fiery prophet based his attack on the failure of the people to take seriously the Sinai covenant, Micah 3:9–12; 6:1–8.

6 Although in 1 Kings 10 the writer takes great delight in describing the lavish nature of Solomon's building ventures, 1 Kings 14:23–25 points out that, five years after Solomon's death, the Egyptians plundered Jerusalem and the Temple, stripped these buildings of their gold and treasures, and took them as booty back to Egypt. So much for the splendor of Solomon's reign!

7 Although Solomon is commonly referred to in popular literature for his wisdom and great building ventures (he built the ***Temple***, *top left*), the truth is that he exploited and enslaved his people (***person carries heavy burden***, *lower right*), particularly those living in the northern part of his realm, to satisfy his personal ambitions and comfort level (***crowned king***, ***submissive figures***, *center right*).

8 ***Women***, ***idols***, ***question marks***: 1 Kings 11:3 states that Solomon had 700 wives and 300 concubines. No doubt, many of these marriages were undertaken to establish and maintain political relationships

Frame 10 (continued)

2

with neighboring nations. The writer never attacks Solomon for having numerous wives; he attacks him for worshiping the false gods of those wives, 1 King 11:1–8. The question marks ask, "Was Solomon really so wise?"

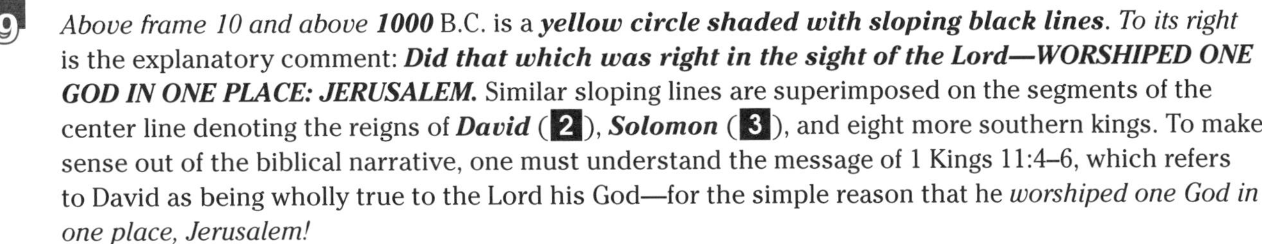

9 *Above frame 10 and above* ***1000*** B.C. is a ***yellow circle shaded with sloping black lines****. To its right is the explanatory comment:* ***Did that which was right in the sight of the Lord—WORSHIPED ONE GOD IN ONE PLACE: JERUSALEM.*** Similar sloping lines are superimposed on the segments of the center line denoting the reigns of ***David*** (2), ***Solomon*** (3), and eight more southern kings. To make sense out of the biblical narrative, one must understand the message of 1 Kings 11:4–6, which refers to David as being wholly true to the Lord his God—for the simple reason that he *worshiped one God in one place, Jerusalem!*

Note also the reference to 1 Samuel 13:14, where the soon-to-be-anointed David is referred to as a person "after God's own heart." The term does not refer to any moral superiority on David's part. It means simply that David would, and did, worship one God in one city, Jerusalem. Hence, any successor who paid special attention to the Jerusalem Temple (which David's son, Solomon, built) is described as one who did what was right, who walked in the way of David his father, and departed neither to the right nor to the left; see 2 Kings 22:2.

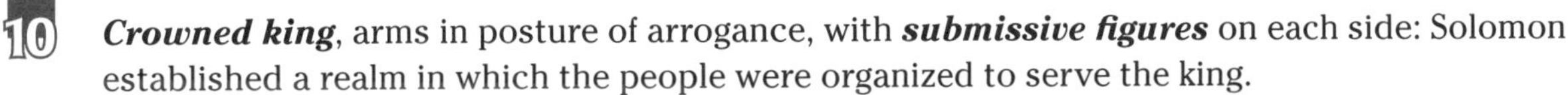

10 ***Crowned king***, arms in posture of arrogance, with ***submissive figures*** on each side: Solomon established a realm in which the people were organized to serve the king.

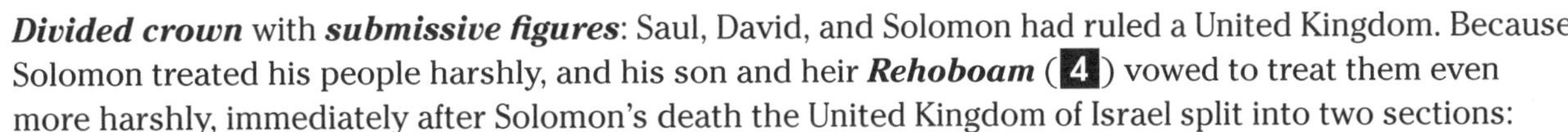

11 ***Divided crown*** with ***submissive figures***: Saul, David, and Solomon had ruled a United Kingdom. Because Solomon treated his people harshly, and his son and heir ***Rehoboam*** (4) vowed to treat them even more harshly, immediately after Solomon's death the United Kingdom of Israel split into two sections:

- The Northern Kingdom of ***ISRAEL***.
- The Southern Kingdom of ***JUDAH***.

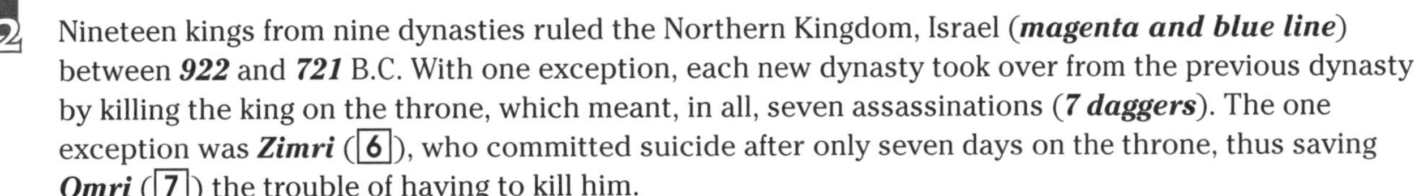

12 Nineteen kings from nine dynasties ruled the Northern Kingdom, Israel (***magenta and blue line***) between ***922*** and ***721*** B.C. With one exception, each new dynasty took over from the previous dynasty by killing the king on the throne, which meant, in all, seven assassinations (***7 daggers***). The one exception was ***Zimri*** (6), who committed suicide after only seven days on the throne, thus saving ***Omri*** (7) the trouble of having to kill him.

After Solomon's death, a total of nineteen kings and one queen (Athaliah) ruled Judah. Although five of these rulers were assassinated (***5 daggers***), the assassination never meant a change in dynasty; the same Davidic family continued to rule. To be specific, ***Jehu*** (11) of the Northern Kingdom killed ***Ahaziah*** (9). The queen mother, ***Athaliah*** (10), a daughter of King ***Ahab*** (8) and Queen Jezebel of Israel), then killed her grandchildren and grabbed the throne. However, unbeknown to Athaliah, one of her grandsons, ***J(eh)oash*** (11), was hidden away in the Temple by the High Priest, Jehoiada, and his wife Jehosheba (Joash's aunt). The people of the land eventually killed Athaliah, replaced her with Joash, but eventually killed Joash and his son ***Amaziah*** (12), and finally Manasseh's son, ***Amon*** (18).

13 The Northern Kingdom of ***ISRAEL*** was eventually destroyed by the Assyrians in ***721*** B.C. To destroy the national identity of those remaining in the northern realm, the Assyrians inter-married them with people brought in from surrounding nations.

14 The Davidic dynasty continued until the Southern Kingdom of ***JUDAH*** was destroyed by the Babylonians in ***587*** B.C. The second-to-last king, ***Jehoiachin*** (22), died in Babylon some time after 560 B.C. In 2 Kings 25:27–30, reference is made to the thirty-seventh year of the exile of Jehoiachin, who was taken to Babylon in ***597*** B.C. Whoever wrote those words must have written them during or after the year 560 B.C.

Frame 11

1 Frame 11 depicts the general thrust of the prophetic attack prior to the destruction of Judah and Jerusalem by the Babylonians in ***587*** B.C. Today, many believe that the ancient prophets merely foretold the future. Although they did some of that, the prophets were *forth*-tellers rather than *fore*-tellers. In other words, they *spoke forth* for God to the people of their own time, and attacked them on the basis of the ***Sinai covenant*** (***shown broken***, *lower left*).

2 The biblical materials state that when the spirit of God came upon the Old Testament prophets (Ezekiel 3:12), they—with a wind in their beards and a fire in their eyes—told kings, leaders, and "professional" priests and prophets that they were to live under the Sinai covenant and serve the nation in a manner in keeping with that covenant's spirit and stipulations. They told their hearers—both the leaders and the common people—that they had forgotten God's goodness and mercy, and charged them with serving personal whims rather than God's will, Hosea 13:4–6.

- They robbed each other in business dealings, Amos 8:4–6 (***scales***). All that the political and religious leaders worried about was how much money they could make for themselves, Micah 3:9–11 (***mouth***, ***dollar sign***). Those in charge of the legal system exploited the poor to fill their own pockets, Amos 5:10,11 (***gavel***, ***dollar sign***).
- Although God was merciful and patient, there was a limit to God's patience. God would maul them like a lion, like a ***leopard***, like a bear robbed of her cubs, Hosea 13:7,8. God would permit the Egyptians, Assyrians, and Babylonians to ravage their land, fortresses, cities, towns, and homes, Hosea 9:6; Jeremiah 27:1–6 (buildings reduced to ***rubble***).
- At the same time, the prophets expressed the hope that, after disciplining the nation, God would make a new beginning to their history as God's people. They hoped that God would make a new covenant with His people and write it on their hearts (***symbol for covenant***, ***heart***, *lower right*) so that they might be a people who truly *knew* their God, Jeremiah 31:31–34.

Frame 12

Despite the hopes and dreams of ***ISRAEL*** and ***JUDAH***, and the beliefs each entertained about its destiny in relation to God's covenant and plan, both nations were eventually destroyed (***city in flames***), and their leaders and many citizens were led into exile (***figures tied to each other***) into foreign lands (***ziggurat***).

Assyria (*profile of Assyrian king*)

1 The ***first magenta-colored section*** in the *horizontal line along the upper edge* of the time-line denotes the Assyrian Empire. One of the reasons Saul, David, and Solomon were able to achieve what they did was that they did not have to cope with any real threats from the Egyptians to the south or from the Assyrians to the north.

2 However, as time went by, the Assyrians began to flex their muscles. Eventually, they made the Northern Kingdom a vassal nation, destroyed it in ***721*** B.C., and scattered many of its citizens around their vast Empire—hence the ***red arrow going upward from Israel*** into a ***circle of chains***, 2 Kings 17. To force captives to cooperate when being led into exile, the Assyrians ran a ***fish hook*** through the nose of each person, and linked the hooks together with cord.

3 The Assyrians inter-married the Israelites they left behind with non-Israelites brought in from around their extensive empire. These "mixed bloods" became known as the *Samaritans*. The Samaritans accepted the *Pentateuch* (Genesis—Deuteronomy) as their Scriptures, believed in the same God as the Jews, but worshiped God on *Mt. Gerizim*—not on *Mt. Zion* in *Jerusalem*. In Jesus' conversation with the woman of Samaria, reference is made to these rival worship places, John ch. 4; see also Luke 9:51–56.

Babylon (*ziggurat*)

1 By the time of the death of ***Shalmaneser V*** ([12]) in 627 B.C., the Assyrian Empire was hearing its own death rattle. The Babylonians finally conquered Assyria, overthrowing Ashur in 614 B.C., and Nineveh in ***612*** B.C. Although the Egyptians gained control of Judah in 609 B.C., in ***605*** B.C. the Babylonians defeated Egypt in battle, and Judah became a vassal of Babylon.

2 King ***Jehoiakim*** ([21]) of Judah revolted against Babylon in 601 B.C. King ***Nebuchadnezzar*** ([18]) of Babylon crushed this revolt in ***597*** B.C. After King ***Zedekiah*** ([23]) of Judah revolted in 589 B.C., Nebuchadnezzar finally destroyed Judah, Jerusalem, the Temple, and the Ark of the Covenant in ***587*** B.C., 2 Kings chs. 24,25. Although the Babylonians left some people in Judah, they took the royal family and thousands of the nobility and leading citizens into exile in Babylon; hence, the ***red arrow from Judah*** to the ***circle of chains*** around Babylon.

3 The Persians under ***Cyrus*** ([23]) captured Babylon in ***539*** B.C., and replaced the Babylonian Empire as the dominant power in the Fertile Crescent. Cyrus pursued an enlightened policy. He permitted captive peoples to return to their homeland, and to rebuild their communities and temples. Hence, the exiles from Judah began to return to their homeland in ***538*** B.C.; note the ***red arrow from Babylon to Judah***. Those who returned to Judah were eventually called *Judeans*, or *Jews* for short. They began and developed that system of belief known still today as ***JUDAISM*** (*beneath the marker for* ***300*** B.C.).

Frame 13

1 Those taken into exile in Babylon experienced an agony of spirit (***sorrowful faces***). They were being forced to live away from what they thought of as the Holy Land (***yellow circle***), the Holy City, and the Holy Temple. They were being forced to sing the Lord's song in a strange land, Psalm 137.

2 Many of them came to understand that they had truly deserved what had overtaken them, for they had indeed broken God's covenant with them. A prophet pointed out that through their suffering, healing and salvation would ultimately flow out to all peoples (***concentric circles radiate out from Holy Land***). God had formed Israel to be a servant community (***servant figure****, lower right*), through whom the light of God's truth (***lamp***) would be made known to the nations, Isaiah 42:1–4, 49:1–6; 50:4–11; 52:13–53:12.

Frame 14

2

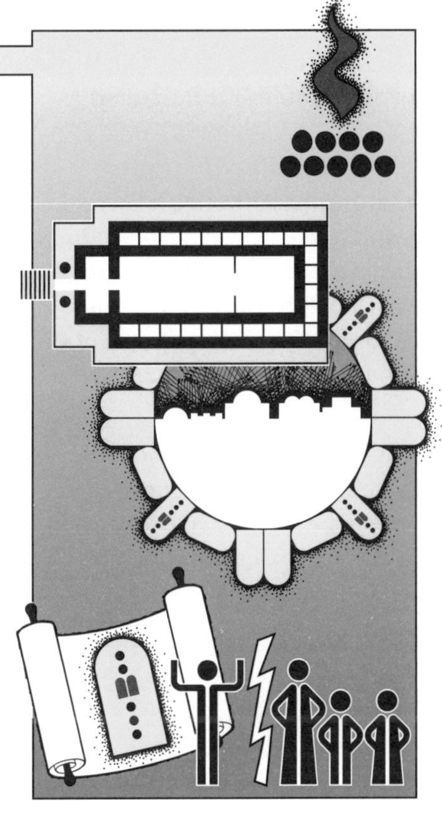

Those who went back from Babylon to Judah imagined that the land to which they would return would be virtually a new Garden of Eden, and that they would experience the Messianic Age within its borders. However, upon their return they did not find a Garden of Eden or a Messianic Age; they found only a mess.

Because Jerusalem, the Temple, and the towns of Judah were in ruins, the people had to undertake the slow, laborious task of rebuilding them and reestablishing themselves as a community within Judah. They had to do that for a variety of obvious reasons—because there was only one God, and because only the Jews knew and belonged to that God, they were duty-bound to make that God known to the nations.

1 ***Altar***: The exiles began to return from Babylon to Judah in ***538*** B.C. One of the first things they did was to build an altar amidst the ruins of Jerusalem, and begin offering sacrifices, Ezra 3:1–6.

2 ***Temple:*** The prophets Haggai and Zechariah (chs. 1–8) urged the returning exiles to rebuild the Jerusalem Temple. The structure was dedicated in ***515*** B.C., Ezra 6:13–18.

3 ***Bricks in circle around Jerusalem skyline:*** Nehemiah spearheaded the move to rebuild Jerusalem's walls, Nehemiah chs. 2,3. He also arranged for more people to live in Jerusalem (ch. 11), established laws forbidding the rich and powerful to exploit the poor (5:1–13), and reinstituted Sabbath observance, 13:15–22.

4 ***Symbols for covenant and commandments in circle around Jerusalem;*** also ***scroll with symbol for covenant:*** The postexilic community became increasingly narrow in its territorial, national, and religious outlook. After Ezra returned from Persia to Jerusalem, he instructed the people in the law of the Lord, and conducted a covenant-renewal ceremony, Nehemiah 8:1–12.

5 ***Fragmentation symbol between man and woman with children:*** Although Nehemiah had forbidden Jewish men to contract marriages with non-Jewish women, he did not nullify any existing Jewish-Gentile marriages, Nehemiah 13:23–29. However, Ezra insisted that all Jewish men married to non-Jewish women dissolve those marriages, and send their Gentile wives and their children away from the restored Jewish community, Ezra chs. 9,10. The intention was to ensure the religious purity of the postexilic community by removing foreign elements. The people remembered only too well how Solomon's many foreign wives had influenced the spiritual life of the nation, 1 Kings 11:1–8.

6 The peoples and nations surrounding Judah generally resented the Jews' attempt to reestablish themselves in the land, and harassed them, Nehemiah 4.

1 ***Symbol for God*, *crown*, *question mark*:** King ***Jehoiakim*** (21) of Judah, who revolted against Babylon in about 601 B.C., died approximately three months before Jerusalem fell in ***597*** B.C. He was succeeded by his 18 year-old son, ***Jehoiachin*** (22), whom ***Nebuchadnezzar*** (18) took into exile. Although many of the exiles hoped that Jehoiachin would live through the exile, return to Jerusalem, and reestablish David's dynasty and borders (2 Kings 25:27–30), Jehoiachin died in Babylon—as did also his successor, ***Zedekiah*** (23), who was forced to watch the execution of his sons, and was then blinded and taken into exile in ***587*** B.C.

2 The postexilic community had no king—apart from God who ruled the people through the priests, and maintained fellowship with them through the rituals the priests performed in the rebuilt Jerusalem Temple. Even so, many in the postexilic community continued to hope that God would eventually restore the Davidic dynasty.

3 Although the postexilic community was able to reestablish itself as a people within the land, and to rebuild Jerusalem, and its walls and Temple, they did not have political independence. They remained vassals, in turn, of the Persians (***winged cherub***), the Greeks, Ptolemies, and Seleucids (***helmet***, ***sword***), and finally of the Romans. To complicate matters, their Greek overlords (including the ***PTOLEMIES***, and in particular the ***SELEUCIDS***) made efforts to impose on the Jews their own Hellenistic culture and way of life (***column***). Little wonder, then, that the agonizing cry went up, "Oh Lord, when will you restore David's dynasty and kingdom?" (See Psalm 89.)

Frame 16

1 The names of many of Israel's prophets are listed in the time-line, beginning with ***ELIJAH*** and ***ELISHA***. Although the ministries of Elijah and Elisha (900–800 B.C.) are reported in 1 Kings 17–2 Kings 10, no writings bearing their names have come down to us.

2 ①–⑫ The literary prophets listed are ***Amos*** ①, ***Hosea*** ②, ***Isaiah*** ③ of Jerusalem, ***Micah*** ④, ***Nahum*** ⑤, ***Habakkuk*** ⑥, ***Zephaniah*** ⑦, ***Jeremiah*** ⑧, and ***Ezekiel*** ⑨—in that order and all prior to the Babylonian exile or during its first years. Jeremiah began his work in 626 B.C., and was still active in ***582*** B.C. Ezekiel was called in 593 B.C. while in Babylon, and his final oracle is dated about 571 B.C.

3 Next comes the book that is usually referred to as Second Isaiah (and *possibly* a Third Isaiah), followed by ***Haggai*** ⑩, ***Zechariah*** ⑪, and ***Malachi*** ⑫. (The names of Obadiah, Joel, and Jonah are not listed on the time-line.) Then, no more literary prophets. Why not?

4 Frame 16 provides the answer. The Jews became *the people of the book*. They believed that there was no further need for the voice of a living prophet. Information about everything they needed to know, believe, and do was now available in their written scriptures (***open scroll***). *Rabbis* (teachers) studied these writings in great detail. As time went by, they produced supplementary writings to explain the law-codes, and apply them to the daily life of the people. Hence, the open scroll contains a center block of inspired writing, around which are interpretive comments by Jewish scholars (***red arrows*** from ***outer interpretive comments*** to ***central inspired text***). See also Zechariah 13:2–6.

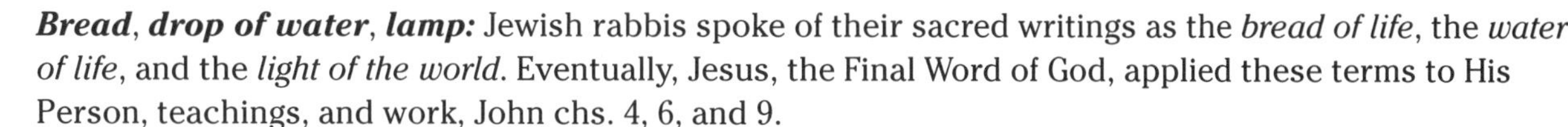

5 ***Bread***, ***drop of water***, ***lamp:*** Jewish rabbis spoke of their sacred writings as the *bread of life*, the *water of life*, and the *light of the world*. Eventually, Jesus, the Final Word of God, applied these terms to His Person, teachings, and work, John chs. 4, 6, and 9.

Frame 17

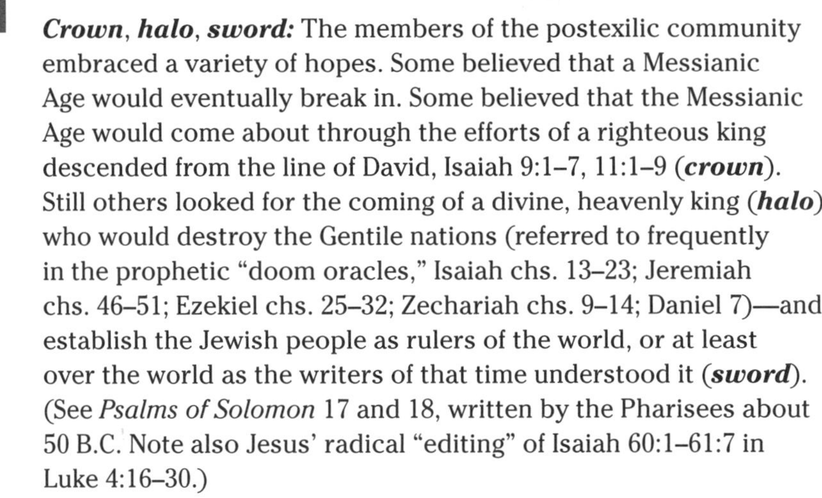

1 ***Crown*, *halo*, *sword:*** The members of the postexilic community embraced a variety of hopes. Some believed that a Messianic Age would eventually break in. Some believed that the Messianic Age would come about through the efforts of a righteous king descended from the line of David, Isaiah 9:1–7, 11:1–9 (***crown***). Still others looked for the coming of a divine, heavenly king (***halo***) who would destroy the Gentile nations (referred to frequently in the prophetic "doom oracles," Isaiah chs. 13–23; Jeremiah chs. 46–51; Ezekiel chs. 25–32; Zechariah chs. 9–14; Daniel 7)—and establish the Jewish people as rulers of the world, or at least over the world as the writers of that time understood it (***sword***). (See *Psalms of Solomon* 17 and 18, written by the Pharisees about 50 B.C. Note also Jesus' radical "editing" of Isaiah 60:1–61:7 in Luke 4:16–30.)

2 ***Arrows pointing to Israel:*** Some within Judaism believed that, when the Messianic Age broke in, Jewish people scattered around the Near Eastern world would return to Israel to take part in that grand, climactic period of history.

3 ***Slatted door,*** signifying resurrection, with ***approval sign:*** The Pharisees, whose origins can be traced to the *Hasidim* who appear on the stage of history about 160 B.C., believed that, when the Messianic Age broke in, the righteous dead would return to life to take part in it, Isaiah 25:8, 26:19; Daniel 12:1–3.

4 ***Slatted door***, signifying resurrection, with ***rejection sign***: The Sadducees, whose origins can also be traced to about 160 B.C., did not believe in any future Messianic Age or the resurrection of the body, Acts 23:8.

Frame 18

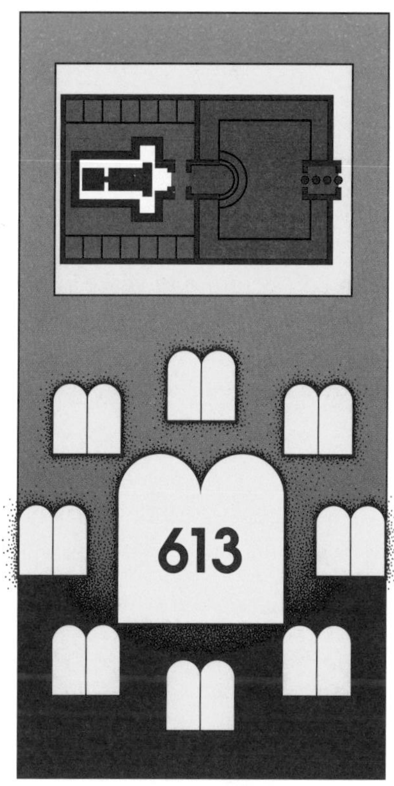

1 ***Temple:*** The postexilic Temple was dedicated in ***515*** B.C. In ***19*** B.C., King ***Herod*** the Great, with the approval of Jewish religious and political leaders, demolished the existing building and replaced it with one of magnificent proportions. The structure, completed in A.D. 63, was destroyed by the Romans in A.D. ***70***.

2 ***Law-code with "613" superimposed:*** According to tradition, the law-codes in the first five books of the Old Testament (the *Pentateuch*) were given to the Israelites while they were living in the Sinai wilderness after leaving Egypt. These consisted of the original Ten Commandments (or "words"), plus an additional 603 commandments that rabbis, or teachers, found in these writings—making a total of ***613***.

3 ***Smaller law-codes around the larger law-code:*** Because the people felt the need to make these law-codes relevant to their new and ever-changing situation, scribes adapted and reinterpreted them for later generations. In due course, there developed a collection of oral teachings known as the traditions of the scribes and Pharisees.

Hundreds of years later, these oral traditions were written down in several collections of writings: The *Mishnah*, *Gemara*, *Tosefta*, *Midrashim*, and the *Talmuds*. The *Palestinian Talmud*, produced at Tiberias, was completed about A.D. 400, and the *Babylonian Talmud* was completed about A.D. 500. The Babylonian Talmud is much larger than the Palestinian Talmud, and is viewed as being more scholarly and having greater authority.

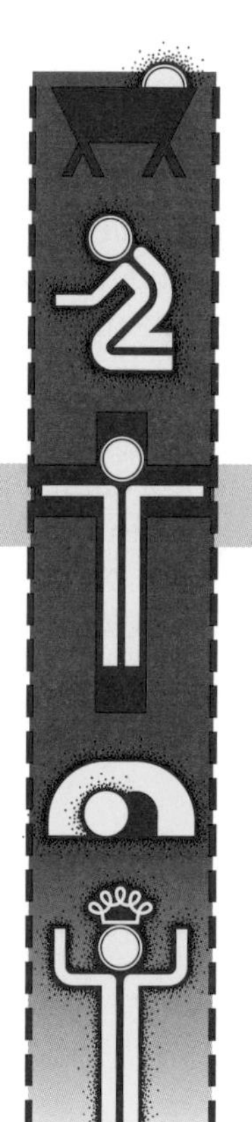

Frame 19

Jesus, the Pivotal Point of Biblical History

Finally, the events outlined in the New Testament began to unfold. On the *vertical strip separating the Old Testament* (***O.T.***) *from the New Testament* (***N.T.***) *sections* of the time-line are symbols of Jesus' birth (***manger***), ***servant*** life, crucifixion (***cross***), burial (***tomb***), resurrection (***open tomb***), and Lordship (***crowned Jesus***).

Frame 20

2

Jesus, complete with ***basin*** and ***towel***, is depicted as a ***Servant-King*** surrounded by a ***community***. This illustration is based on a number of biblical passages:

1 The words spoken at Jesus' baptism: "You are my Son, the Beloved; with you I am well pleased," Mark 1:9–11.

"You are my Son, the Beloved," is found in verse 7 of Psalm 2, a royal psalm. It was used when a king from the line of David was enthroned. Its use at Jesus' baptism declares that Jesus was anointed King of God's people (***crown***).

"With you I am well pleased" is found in Isaiah's first Servant Song, Isaiah 42:1–4. Its use at Jesus' baptism defines the nature of His kingship and kingdom (***Servant-King***).

2 John 13:1–17 states that, during the night prior to His crucifixion, Jesus washed His disciples' feet, and told them that they were to do the same for each other (***basin*** and ***towel***).

3 Around Jesus is a ***community***. During His ministry, Jesus gathered around Himself a group of people. In Jesus' Kingdom, all distinctions between male and female, one race and another, master and servant, were and are declared null and void, and rejected, Gal. 3:28. Jesus' followers are to ask only: **"How can I reflect Jesus' attitude toward the Father, toward the created order, and toward others?"**

4 Above the symbols for Jesus and His community is a ***dove***, the symbol for the Holy Spirit. The risen, ascended Jesus continues among His people through His Holy Spirit. The Spirit uses the Holy scriptures to continue to make known the completed work of Jesus. Their work is one and inseparable, John 16:14,15.

Frame 21

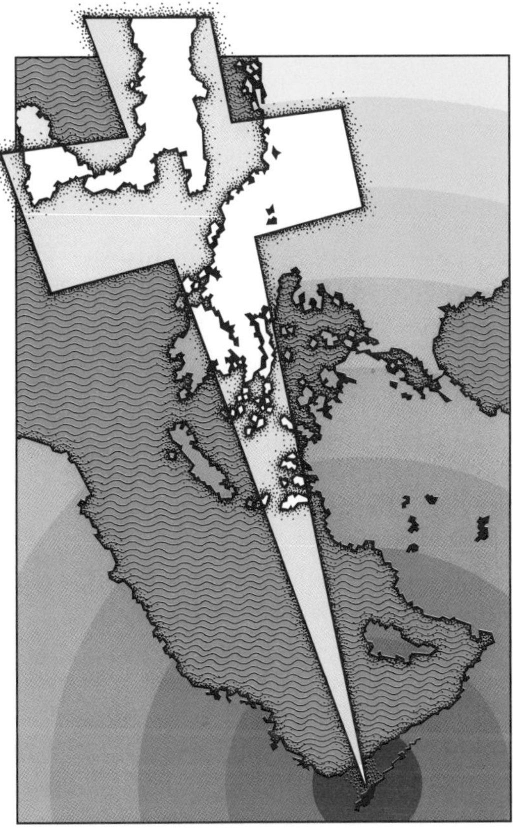

1 Until the very day of Jesus' ascension, the disciples were expecting Jesus to restore the Davidic kingdom—a geographical kingdom that was political in nature. Jesus rejected this expectation, Acts 1:6–8.

2 Furthermore, Jesus told the disciples that the Holy Spirit would soon empower them to witness about Jesus (***cross***) to those living in Jerusalem, Judea, Samaria—and even to the ends of the earth (***concentric circles radiate out from Holy Land***), Acts 1:8.

3 Although many Jews hoped to see a Messianic Age established in Judea and centered in Jerusalem, Jesus sent people away from Jerusalem to distant corners of the then-known world. Although some Jews hoped that even Romans would come to worship the God of the Jews in Jerusalem, at the close of the Book of Acts (ch. 28), Paul is bearing witness to Jesus in Rome. The world would not be won for God by zealot swords, but by the message and mission of a gentle Galilean, Jesus the Messiah.

Frame 22

The New Testament teaches that Jesus the Messiah (***crowned Jesus with extended arms***) will reappear on a day that will mark the close of history, Matthew 25:31–46.

On that day, Jesus will separate humanity into two groups—***sheep*** at His right hand, ***goats*** at His left hand.

He will welcome those at His right hand (those blessed by His Father), and invite them to inherit the kingdom prepared for them from the foundation of the world, Matthew 25:31–40. He will also reject those who claimed to know Him as Lord, but made no effort to demonstrate discipleship by serving others, Matthew 25:41–46. Although the Bible proclaims that salvation is always "by grace, through faith" in Jesus the Messiah, crucified, risen, and reigning, it always attaches the concept of "for works, for servanthood" to "by grace, through faith," Ephesians 2:8–10. Faith in the heart demonstrates itself in service to others through attitudes, words, and actions.

Although Jesus will finally receive people into eternal fellowship with Himself on the basis of the gracious forgiveness of sins, He will commend them for works of service (***two servant figures***) they did to the needy around them—and through them, to Jesus Himself in "distressing disguise." He will thank them for providing for His needs when He was hungry (***plate, knife and fork***), thirsty (***drinking glass***), lonely (***one person separated from three other persons***), lacking ***clothing***, sick (***serpent around staff***—symbol for healing, Numbers 21:1–9) and in prison (***person behind barred window***). Jesus will also reject those who claimed the right to call Him "Lord," but failed to serve Him in His multitude of distressing disguises, Matthew 25:41–46.

Meal, signified by food and drink on a table (*left*): Jesus frequently ate with people. In Jesus' day, to eat with people was to accept them warmly as brothers and sisters. It was to establish a sense of sacred community with them. It was to commit life to serving and protecting those who shared in the fellowship of the meal.

Basin and towel (*right*): Jesus performed the duties of a servant for His disciples—He washed their feet. He exhorted them, and exhorts His family today, to copy Him, and to make Him—the present but invisible Jesus—known in all they think, say, and do, John 13:1–17.

Drop of water—baptism (*center*): In Holy Baptism, God declares the person being baptized to be His forgiven child, and to be one who has shared in Jesus' sinless servant life, atoning death, and victory over death and the grave.

Bread and cup (*center*): Prior to His final appearing, Jesus continues among His people, invisibly, through His Spirit. He invites them to share table with Him (as He shared table with His disciples during His earthly ministry), and gives them Himself to eat and drink through visible elements of bread and wine. Those who share sacramental table fellowship with Him are to "become" what they eat. They are to demonstrate in their own lives the life of Jesus, their forgiving Savior and Servant Lord.

And Finally...

2

The following paragraph was written by H.G. Wells. Its implications are timeless.

> *Jesus was too great for His disciples. And in view of what He plainly said, is it any wonder that all who were rich and prosperous felt a horror of strange things, a swimming of their world at His teaching? Perhaps the priests and rulers and rich men understood Him better than His followers. He was dragging out all the little private reservations they had made from social service into the light of a universal religious life. He was like a terrible moral huntsman, digging mankind out of the snug burrows in which they had lived hitherto. In the white blaze of His kingdom there was to be no property, no privilege, no pride and no precedence, no motive and reward but love. Is it any wonder that men were dazzled and blinded, and cried out against Him? Even His disciples cried out when He would not spare them that light. Is it any wonder that the priests realized that between this Man and themselves there was no choice, but that He or their priestcraft should perish? Is it any wonder that the Roman soldiers, confronted and amazed by something soaring over their comprehension and threatening all their disciplines, should take refuge in wild laughter, and crown Him with thorns and robe Him in purple and make a mock Caesar of Him? For to take Him seriously was to enter into a strange and alarming life, to abandon habits, to control instincts and impulses, to essay [embrace] an incredible happiness. Is it any wonder that to this day this Galilean is too much for our small hearts?*
>
> *The Outline of History*, Vol. 1, pp. 425–6

3A

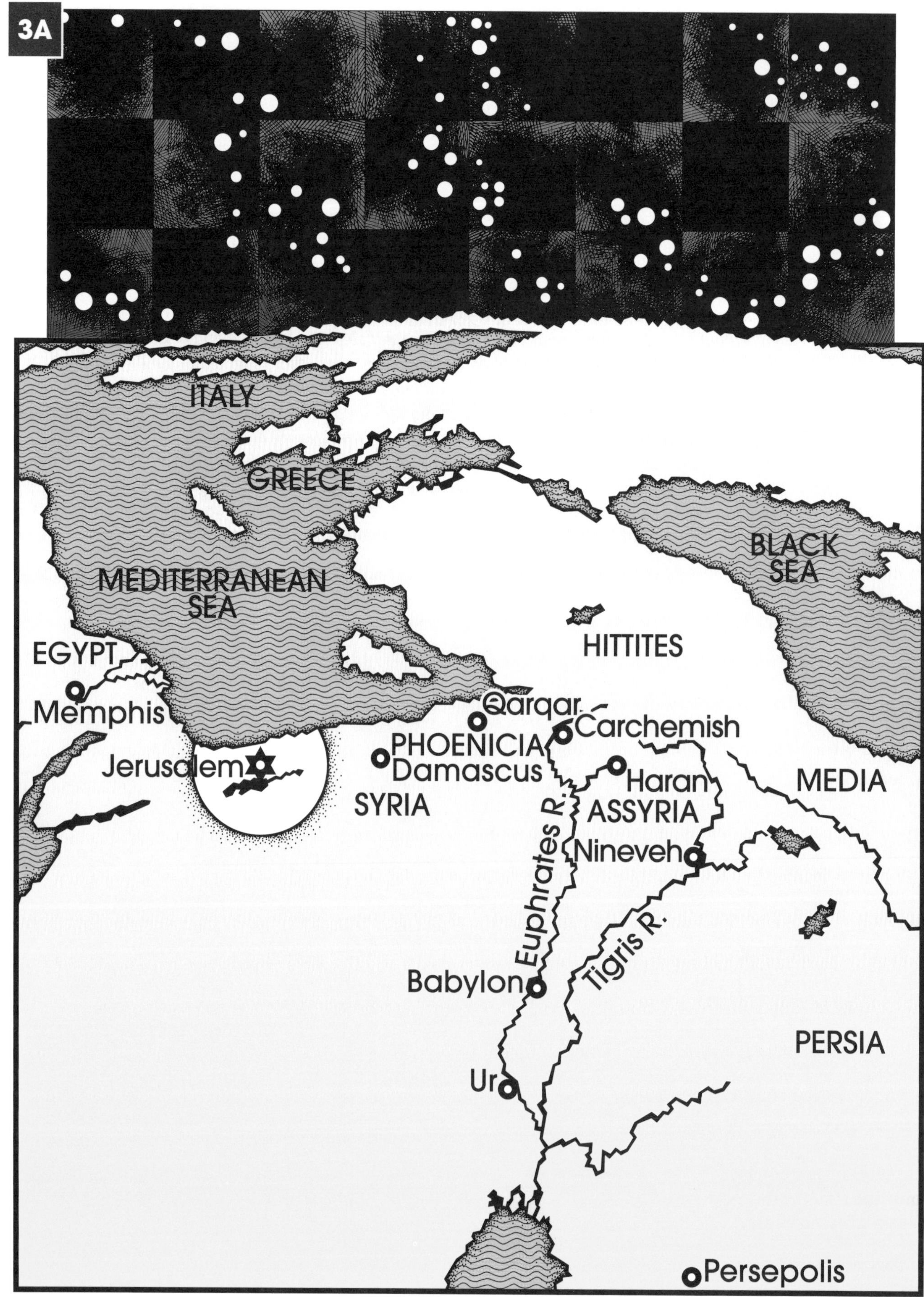
ITALY
GREECE
MEDITERRANEAN SEA
BLACK SEA
HITTITES
EGYPT
Memphis
Jerusalem
Qarqar
Carchemish
PHOENICIA
Damascus
Haran
SYRIA
MEDIA
ASSYRIA
Euphrates R.
Nineveh
Tigris R.
Babylon
PERSIA
Ur
Persepolis

Human Kingdoms—God's Kingdom

3A. The Biblical Stage: Then

It is possible to graduate from Sunday School thinking that the Bible is merely about heroes who lived in a safe, secure land insulated from the history of surrounding nations—heroes who devoted themselves wholeheartedly to the worship and service of God. Not so! The ancient Israelites lived among superpowers that were constantly at war with each other, and some of them worshiped a variety of gods.

ILLUSTRATION 3A depicts "an astronaut's view" of the ***Mediterranean*** world in which the biblical narrative unfolds. (The name *Mediterranean* is derived from two Latin words that mean "in the middle of land.") The land of *Canaan* (***white circle***) is located at "center stage." The *Israelites* who settled in Canaan were the descendants of Abraham, Isaac, and Jacob (later referred to as the *patriarchs*, the *fathers* of the Israelites, the "chosen people"). David captured ***Jerusalem*** and made it his capital, 2 Samuel 5:6–10.

There were usually tensions and troubled relations between the Israelites and ***SYRIA***. Good relations prevailed between the Israelites and ***PHOENICIA***. The Phoenicians were a sea-faring people (the Israelites were not) who played an important role in international trading ventures. The Israelites needed access to their sea-faring skills and services.

The region between the ***Tigris*** and ***Euphrates*** Rivers was known as *Mesopotamia*—a name derived from two Greek words meaning "between the rivers."

The *Assyrians*, *Babylonians*, and *Persians* established successive empires in Mesopotamia. The Babylonians conquered Assyrian ***Nineveh*** in 612 B.C. Cyrus the Persian gained control of ***MEDIA*** in 550 B.C., and conquered ***Babylon*** in 539 B.C. The *Greeks* under Alexander the Great ravaged ***Persepolis***, a major Persian capital city, in 330 B.C. In 40–37 B.C., the *Parthians* (not shown; to the northeast of Media) helped Antigonus, a descendant of the Jewish Hasmonean rulers (165–63 B.C.), gain control of *Judea* and ***Jerusalem***—and block Rome's land-bridge to ***EGYPT***. (The Hasmoneans were descendants of the Maccabees who revolted against Antiochus IV "Epiphanes" of Syria in 165 B.C.)

The ***HITTITES***, Assyrians, Babylonians, Persians, Greeks, and Romans (***ITALY***) consistently cast covetous eyes on Egypt, whose fertile *Nile Valley* was the bread-basket of the ancient Mediterranean world. When these ancient superpowers set out to plunder Egypt's resources, they naturally marched through Canaan along the way. The Mesopotamian nations could not follow a direct route to Egypt, but had to travel "between the rivers" and down the Mediterranean coast—to ensure access to food and water.

The Egyptians were aware of the ambitions and needs of their northern neighbors. To discourage invasions, the Egyptians built a series of fortresses along the Mediterranean coast; the most northern one was located at ***Carchemish***. The Egyptians used these fortresses to block the advance of Mesopotamian nations and discourage the empire-building dreams of southern European powers.

Because nations believed that their gods led them into battle and gave them their victories, they usually placed symbols of the gods of conquered nations in their shrines (1 Samuel 5:1,2), and symbols of their gods in the shrines of those they conquered. This practice declared, "Because we were able to conquer you, our gods are obviously stronger than your gods." In 2 Kings 23:4,5 the references to "the host of heaven" and "the sun, the moon, the constellations, and all the host of the heavens" in the Jerusalem Temple are to Assyrian astral deities.

On occasion, God declared that He would use the armies of other nations, such as Assyria and Babylon, to discipline His own rebellious people; see Isaiah 10:5, Jeremiah 27:6.

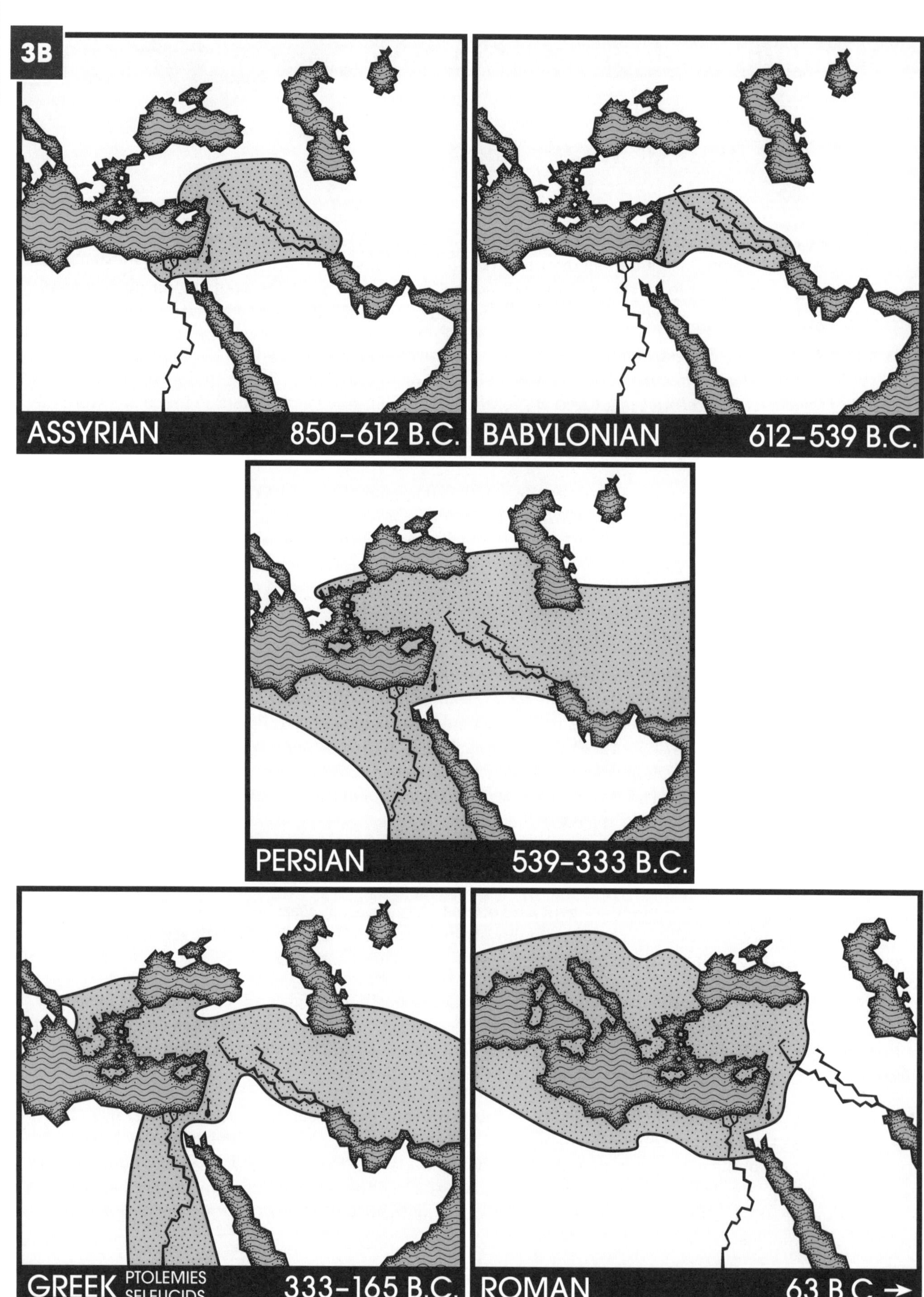
3B
ASSYRIAN
850–612 B.C.
BABYLONIAN
612–539 B.C.
PERSIAN
539–333 B.C.
GREEK
PTOLEMIES
SELEUCIDS
333–165 B.C.
ROMAN
63 B.C.→

3B. Memories and Hopes

The maps in **ILLUSTRATION 3B** depict the five empires that played a key role in the history of ancient Israel. One empire after another took control of Israel and made it part of its empire. The illustration does not depict the roles that Egypt and Syria played in Israel's history.

1 The Assyrian Empire

Assyria was politically active in the Middle East region even before the time of the patriarchs. Fortunately for Israel, Assyrian influence was at its lowest point during the reign of Israel's most popular king, David (1,000–960 B.C.). In due course, Assyria's power increased, and its influence—particularly in the Northern Kingdom of Israel—resulted in that kingdom becoming an Assyrian vassal in 841 B.C. As Assyria's fortunes and power decreased, Israel and Judah gained some freedom and prominence under Jeroboam II and Uzziah. However, in 745 B.C., Tiglath-Pileser III set about restoring Assyria's imperial state, and dealt harshly with Israelite attempts to gain independence. In 721 B.C., the Assyrians overran the Northern Kingdom of Israel, led its people into exile, and brought Israel's history to an end.

2 The Babylonian Empire

The best-known king of the First Babylonian Dynasty (18th century B.C., about the time of Abraham) was Hammurabi, the author of a famous code of laws. During the early part of the first millennium B.C., the Assyrians controlled Babylon. However, the Babylonians threw off the Assyrian yoke in ***612 B.C.***, and dominated Western Asia until ***539 B.C.*** Nebuchadnezzar took the Southern Kingdom of Judah into exile in Babylon in two deportations in 597 and 587 B.C.

3 The Persian Empire

The Persians under Cyrus conquered the Babylonians in ***539 B.C.***, and then went on to develop and control an empire stretching from India to the Aegean Sea and Egypt. The Persian rulers treated captive nations much more kindly than the Assyrians and Babylonians had treated them. Eventually their realm became part of the empire of Alexander the Great.

4 The Greek Empire

After Philip of Macedon was assassinated in 336 B.C., his son Alexander, then only 20 years old, succeeded him. By the time of his death in 323 B.C. at the age of 33, Alexander the Great had conquered much of the Mediterranean world. He died during a campaign in Babylon, but before his death he divided the empire among his generals.

Two generals are of importance for understanding Jewish history: Ptolemy and Seleucus. Ptolemy and his descendants (the ***PTOLEMIES***) gained control of Egypt, and ruled Jewish territory 301–198 B.C. Seleucus and his descendants (the ***SELEUCIDS***) ruled Syria, and gained control of Jewish territory in 198 B.C. The Jews, under the leadership of the Maccabees, began a struggle for freedom from the Seleucids in ***165 B.C.***, and finally won full independence in 142 B.C. The Maccabees established a line of Jewish rulers known as the Hasmoneans. The Hasmoneans were not descendants of David.

5 The Roman Empire

In ***63 B.C.***, the emperor Pompey made Syria (which included Judah) a Roman province. With that move, the Jewish people came under Roman domination for several centuries.

In Jesus' day, the Jews looked for a coming Messiah to deliver them from the Romans. However, the New Testament writers point out that the Romans did not constitute the "real enemy," Matthew 1:21.

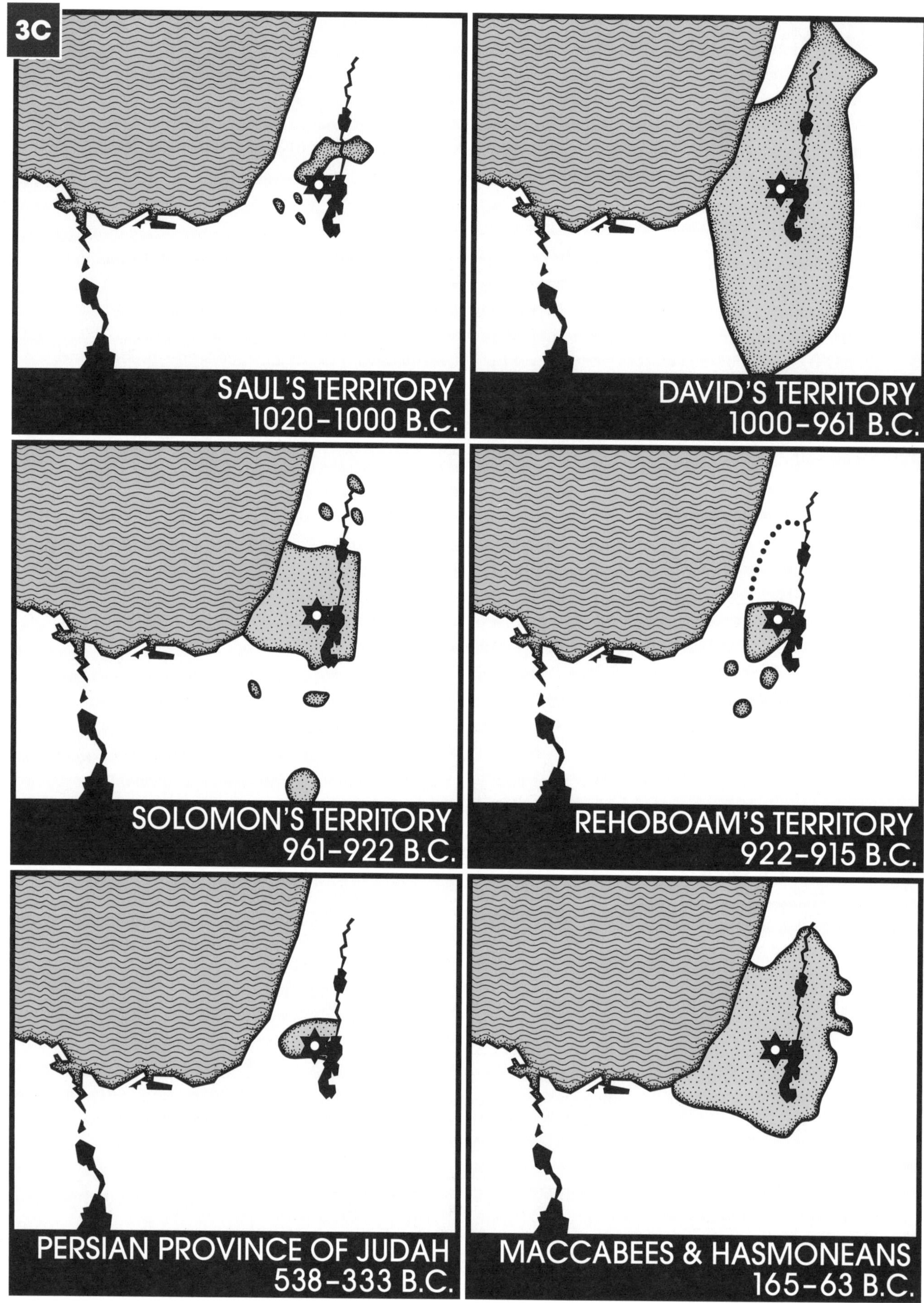
3C
SAUL'S TERRITORY
1020–1000 B.C.
DAVID'S TERRITORY
1000–961 B.C.
SOLOMON'S TERRITORY
961–922 B.C.
REHOBOAM'S TERRITORY
922–915 B.C.
PERSIAN PROVINCE OF JUDAH
538–333 B.C.
MACCABEES & HASMONEANS
165–63 B.C.

3C. Memories and Dreams

3

ILLUSTRATION 3C shows how the nation's borders increased and decreased as its fortunes waxed and waned. The postexilic community hoped that God would one day make their realm as large as David's kingdom had been.

1 Saul's Territory

The size of the realm Saul ruled is uncertain. Although many believe that Saul's kingdom was quite small, 1 Samuel 14:47,48 reports that he carried out numerous punitive campaigns against neighboring nations that had harassed the Israelites. However, this passage does not state that Saul incorporated these regions into his realm.

2 David's Territory

David's realm was large. The memory of what it had once been continued to influence the Jewish people throughout their history, and gave rise to the Zealot revolts against the Romans in A.D. 66–70 and 132–135.

3 Solomon's Territory

There are suggestions that Solomon's realm was even larger than David's, 1 Kings 4:21. However, toward the close of Solomon's reign, his realm decreased in size when the Syrians and Edomites gained their independence, 1 Kings 11:14–25.

4 Rehoboam's Territory

Solomon's son, Rehoboam, gained control only of Judah. The Northern Kingdom was taken over by Jeroboam (1 Kings 11:26–40; 12:1–33) and ruled by nine different dynasties. The Assyrians destroyed it in 721 B.C. After revolts against Babylon by King Jehoiakim and King Zedekiah, many from Judah were taken into exile in Babylon in 597 and 587 B.C. In 538 B.C., many of the exiles in Babylon began to return to Judah.

5 Persian Province of Judah

Postexilic Judah was small, and apart from a short period of independence under the Maccabees and their descendants, the Hasmoneans, it was never free.

6 Maccabees & Hasmoneans

The Maccabees revolted against the Syrians in ***165 B.C.***, and finally gained full independence in 142 B.C. Their descendants, the Hasmoneans, eventually established a realm of considerable size. Some saw the Hasmonean realm as the Messianic Kingdom. Although the Maccabees-Hasmoneans were Levites (the priestly tribe descended from Aaron, a descendant of Levi), they were not descendants of Zadok—a factor which angered many when the Hasmoneans assumed the role of High Priest. (Zadok was David's priest; he anointed Solomon as David's successor, 1 Kings 1:32–48; note also 1 Chronicles 15:11, and the many references to Zadok throughout 1 and 2 Chronicles; see also Ezekiel 40:46, 43:19, 44:15, 48:11.) The level of anger increased when the Hasmoneans combined the role of High Priest with that of king. *Only descendants of David could be legitimate kings!* In ***63 B.C.***, the Romans took control of Judah.

For hundreds of years, many within Judaism hoped that one day God would restore the Davidic kingdom. Up to the very moment of Jesus' ascension, even Jesus' disciples shared that hope, Acts 1:6.

3D

3D. The Nature of the Messianic Kingdom

1 Some believe that the Old Testament people of God were to save themselves by obedience to the commandments given at Sinai. This is not true. Salvation has always been *by grace, through faith* in God's merciful forgiveness of sins—a faith that expresses itself in obedience to God. The word *grace* weaves its way all through the Old Testament.

2 During the period between the Testaments, some within Judaism did believe that salvation *was* earned *by works*. They viewed the commandments as a *merit system* rather than as a *response system*.

3 The issue at stake in the Gospels is: What kind of a Messiah was Jesus? What was the nature of Jesus' Kingship? What kind of kingdom did Jesus establish? Although the Jews were waiting for a Messiah, they were not expecting the lifestyle of the Messiah to be that of a servant.

4 **ILLUSTRATION 3D** draws on John 13:1–17 to portray the nature of Jesus' Messiahship. It shows ***Jesus on His knees washing Peter's feet***.

- At His baptism Jesus was declared to be *King* ("You are my Son, the Beloved," Mark 1:11; see Psalm 2:7. Psalm 2 is a royal coronation psalm) and *Servant* ("with you I am well pleased," Mark 1:11; see Isaiah 42:1; Isaiah 42:1–4 is a "servant song"). Symbols pointing to these truths are at the *center* of the illustration (***Servant-King***).
- Also included are symbols of Jesus' crucifixion and resurrection (***cross*** and ***open tomb***). When Jesus went to the cross, He went there as **the Servant without limit**. None who witnessed Jesus' trial and crucifixion expected Him to return to life. However, Jesus' Father raised Him from the dead and, in so doing, gave **the deciding vote that declared Jesus to be the Messiah!**
- Around the symbols depicting Jesus' ministry is a ***circle of people holding hands in community***. **God's desire is that all live in community, seeking to glorify God and serve each other in all they do.** Unlike most humans, God is not interested in national borders, flags, and skin colors—or in any of the other ways in which people subdivide the human family.

5 God sends the Holy Spirit (***dove***) to help people understand, believe, and embrace the tremendous truths that relate to Jesus' ministry, and to empower them to live as members of Jesus' servant community.

A verse by George McDonald defines the "surprising" nature of Jesus' kingdom. He wrote:

They were all waiting for a king
to slay their foes and raise them high.
Thou cam'st a little baby thing
that made a woman cry.

To which might be added:

Thou cam'st to do Thy servant thing,
on cruel cross to die

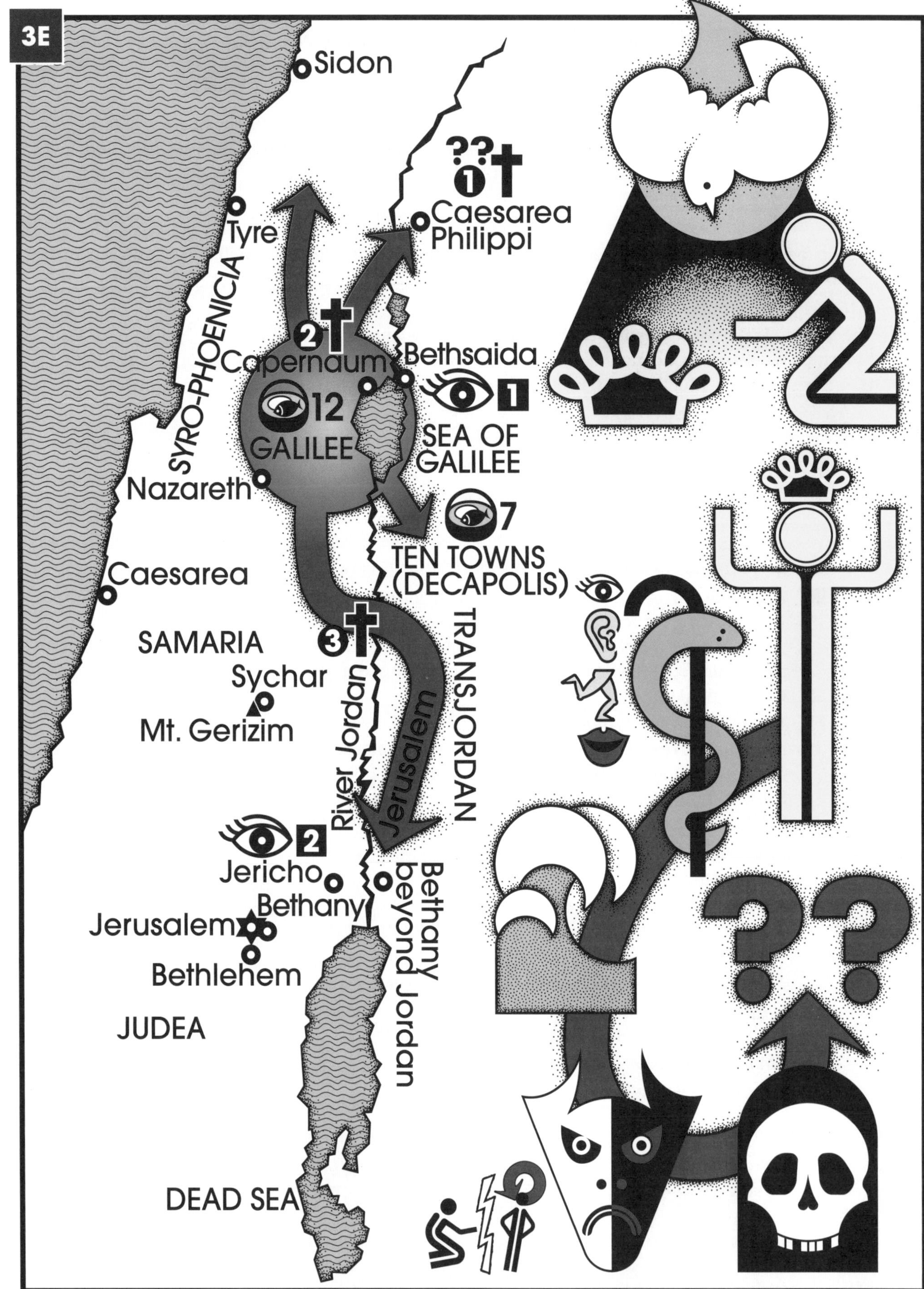
3E
Sidon
Tyre
Caesarea
Philippi
SYRO-PHOENICIA
Capernaum
Bethsaida
12
GALILEE
1
SEA OF
GALILEE
Nazareth
7
TEN TOWNS
(DECAPOLIS)
Caesarea
SAMARIA
3
Sychar
Mt. Gerizim
River Jordan
Jerusalem
TRANSJORDAN
2
Jericho
Bethany
Jerusalem
Bethany
beyond Jordan
Bethlehem
JUDEA
DEAD SEA

3E. Jesus' Ministry in Mark's Gospel

1 Accepting the location for John the Baptist's work as initially ***Bethany beyond Jordan*** (John 1:28), Jesus' baptism and temptation took place somewhere just north of the ***DEAD SEA***, Mark 1:1–13. After Jesus was baptized, He found Himself face to face with the demonic (***satanic face***), 1:12,13—a confrontation and battle which continued all the way to the cross, where Jesus emerged the victor.

2 The bulk of Jesus' ministry took place in ***GALILEE*** itself, Mark 1:14–7:23. However, during this period, He did cross the ***SEA OF GALILEE*** and minister on its eastern shore, Mark 5:1–20. Jesus also ministered in non-Jewish territory such as ***SYRO-PHOENICIA*** (Mark 7:24–30), and the ***DECAPOLIS***, 7:31–8:10.

3 Jesus needed time to make clear to His followers the message that He was indeed the Messiah—but not the kind of Messiah that the disciples and the people-at-large were expecting. In doing this, Jesus revealed His Messianic identity through *actions* rather than *words*.

a. ***Serpent around staff***, *a symbol of healing*, Numbers 21:9. Isaiah had written that when the Messianic Age broke in, the blind would see (***eye***), the deaf would hear (***ear***), the crippled would walk (***moving legs***), and the dumb would speak (***mouth***); see Isaiah 35:5,6. Jesus did those very things. He gave sight to the *blind*, hearing to the *deaf*, healthy bodies to the *crippled*, and speech to the *dumb*; see Mark 8:22–26 and 10:46–52; Mark 7:31–37; Mark 2:1–12.

b. ***White-capped waves:*** The Jewish people were not a sea-faring people. They were, by and large, afraid of the oceans and storms at sea. They took comfort in the fact that God could control the oceans, the storms, and the winds, Psalms 89:9, 107:23–32. Jesus stilled the storms (Mark 4:35–41), and walked on the waters—thereby demonstrating His deity, power, and authority, Mark 6:45–52; John 6:16–21.

c. ***Demonic face:*** The Old Testament contains only a few references to Satan (e.g., 1 Chronicles 21:1). Jesus, as it were, flushed out the reality of the demonic, teaching that the demonic is every spirit, power, institution, and pressure that diverts people from living to serve God and others into living to serve themselves. Jesus taught that His followers are involved in a non-stop, lifelong holy war—against the "deadly trio" of the demonic, the world order around them, and the sinful, "serve-self" desires of the human heart.

d. ***Tombstone with skull***, *symbolizing death:* A number of Old Testament passages state that, when the Messianic Age broke in, the dead would be raised, Isaiah 25:8, 26:19, Daniel 12:1–3. In raising the dead (Mark 5:21–24a, 35–43; Luke 7:11–17; John ch. 11), Jesus demonstrated that the Messianic Age had broken in!

4 Mark reports two feeding miracles. After Jesus feeds 5,000 Jews in Galilee (6:30–44), there are 12 baskets of leftovers (***basket containing fish and bread***, ***12***)—perhaps one basket for each of the 12 tribes refered to in the Old Testament. After Jesus feeds 4,000 Gentiles in the non-Jewish Decapolis region (8:1–10, ***basket containing fish and bread***, ***7***), there are seven baskets of leftovers. Several Old Testament passages list seven Gentile nations who live on Israel's borders and whom the "Chosen People" hate; Deuteronomy 7:1, Ezekiel chs. 25–32.

5 After working in the Decapolis, Jesus headed north toward ***Caesarea Philippi***. Along the way, He healed a blind man in two stages at ***Bethsaida***, Mark 8:22–26 (***eye***, **1**). After leaving Bethsaida, Jesus began openly asking the disciples who the people-at-large, and who they themselves, thought He was, Mark 8:27–30. Peter, speaking on behalf of the disciples, said that although the people-at-large thought that Jesus was John the Baptist or Elijah come back to life, or a prophet, the disciples had come to the

conclusion that Jesus was the Messiah, Mark 8:29. Jesus told them to say nothing to anyone about Him, Mark 8:30.

6 Jesus then predicted for the first time His coming passion in Jerusalem, Mark 8:31 (❶, ***cross, two question marks***). The disciples responded with disbelief, Mark 8:32. A Messiah who would finish up on a cross did not appeal to them! Jesus rebuked the disciples for their attitude, and proceeded to explain what it meant to be involved with Him, Mark 8:34–38. (See also 9:30–32, 10:32–34.)

7 The cycle of (1) prediction, (2) confusion, and (3) clarification took place again a few miles further south, just north of Capernaum, 9:30–35 (❷, ***cross***). Jesus predicted His passion. The disciples did not get the message. When the group entered a house in Capernaum and Jesus asked the disciples what they had been talking about, they said nothing—they were ashamed to admit that they had been discussing who was, and would be, "Number One!" among them. Jesus told them that, in His kingdom, those who aspire to be *first* must strive to be *last* and the servant of everybody else! Another shock for the disciples!

8 Jesus then left Galilee and headed south toward ***Jerusalem***, Mark 10:1. It happened again! There was a prediction (10:32–34), confusion (10:35–40), and clarification, 10:41–45 (❸, ***cross***). This time James and John asked to be granted a special favor: At Jesus' enthronement in Jerusalem, they wanted the honor of sitting immediately to Jesus' right and left in the coronation ceremony! Jesus informed the disciples that, in His Kingdom, things were different from the way they are in earthly kingdoms! In the world, greatness is measured by how many people serve you; in His Kingdom greatness is measured by how many people you serve. Without doubt, the disciples were now thinking, "This is not what we had in mind!"

9 Further along the way, in the vicinity of ***Jericho***, Jesus healed another blind man, Mark 10:46–52 (***eye***, **2**). Initially, the first incident (8:22–26) strikes readers as a little strange. People brought a blind man to Jesus and begged Him to touch the man. Jesus responded by taking the blind man by the hand and leading him out of the village. Jesus then put saliva on the man's eyes, laid His hands on him, and asked, "Can you see anything?" The man replied that he could see, but things looked rather blurry. People, for example, looked like walking trees. Jesus touched the man's eyes a second time, and the man's sight was restored completely.

Jesus' actions in healing this first blind man reflected the fact that, although the disciples could "see" that Jesus was the Messiah, but they could not "see" what that would finally mean for *Jesus*—and for *them*. They needed a "second touch." Their eyes would be fully opened only after Jesus' resurrection (16:7, "see").

10 The second incident appears less complex. As Jesus and the disciples left Jericho and headed for Jerusalem, they passed by a blind beggar, Bartimaeus, sitting at the side of the road. Remarkably, although Bartimaeus was blind, he could "see" who Jesus was. He called out, "Jesus, *Son of David*, have mercy on me!" After Jesus restored his sight, Bartimaeus responded by following Jesus. His joy would have been a sight to behold!

Jesus continued on His way to Jerusalem, and—five days after entering the city—was crucified and buried. In light of Jesus' resurrection several days later, we too must ask, in the spirit of Pilate's questions in John's trial narrative, "Just Who is it that we are involved with? Where is He from? What has He done? What does it all mean?" Our answer must be that of Thomas, "My Lord and my God!" (John 20:28).

Understanding the Bible's Key Themes

Explanations of the five illustrations on the reverse side of the Time-Line.

FRAME 1

MY PROPERTY!
HANDLE WITH CARE!
MY PROPERTY AND
INSTRUMENT FOR SERVICE.
DEVELOP,
CARE FOR AND
USE RESPONSIBLY.

FRAME 1: Maker and Owner

ILLUSTRATION FRAME 1 (on the back of the time-line) shows ***Planet Earth*** and a ***human being***, with ***God's ownership label*** attached to each.

Upper section

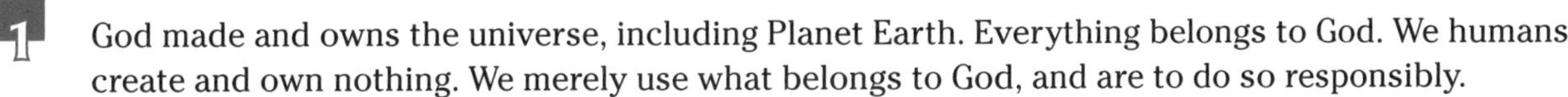

1 God made and owns the universe, including Planet Earth. Everything belongs to God. We humans create and own nothing. We merely use what belongs to God, and are to do so responsibly.

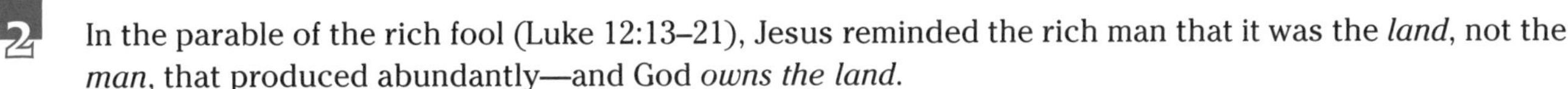

2 In the parable of the rich fool (Luke 12:13–21), Jesus reminded the rich man that it was the *land*, not the *man*, that produced abundantly—and God *owns the land.*

3 There is no such thing as "Christian *giving*." People cannot give what they do not own. God's people are to see themselves as called not to *give more*, but to *rob less*. They are to practice Christian *managing*, *caring*, and *sharing* in all they do.

Lower Section

1 God made and owns *all people* on Planet Earth. Again in Luke 12:13–21, Jesus reminded the rich fool that *his very life was being lent to him by God*, and that very night *God would demand that the rich man's life-on-loan be returned to its Owner. The rich man was about to die!*

2 God has endowed us with faculties and abilities. We are to view these with respect, develop them responsibly and wisely, and use them to glorify God by serving others.

3 Our actions toward others are to reflect God's prior actions toward us, 1 John 4:19–21. We do not love others so that God may love us; we love others to reflect the wonderful truth that God already loves us.

4 **When we live according to God's will reflected in the life of Jesus the Messiah, we find meaning and joy in life, and bring meaning and joy to others.**

FRAME 2

BECAUSE

THEREFORE

FRAME 2: Because I—Therefore You

People do not earn acceptance from God by good deeds. They cannot! God never intended that people even try to do this. All such attempts are misguided and contrary to God's will, Romans 3:27,28.

Throughout the Bible, God first tells people who He is and what He has done for them. Only then does God state what He wishes people to do for Him—that they should serve God by serving others. **ILLUSTRATION FRAME 2** (on the back of the time-line) depicts the biblical sequence: "*Because I* (God)—*therefore you* (humanity)."

Upper section

BECAUSE

Left segment, ***Exodus 1*** (see Deuteronomy 15:15). God rescued the Israelites from slavery in Egypt, and led them through the wilderness into the Promised Land.

Right segment, ***Exodus 2***. The illustration contains symbols of:

- Jesus' life (***Servant-King***)
- Jesus' crucifixion (***cross***)—in reality, Jesus' coronation (***crown above cross***)
- Jesus' resurrection (***open tomb***)
- Jesus' ascension (***arrow rising into cloud***)
- The Holy Spirit (***dove***)

In the original Greek of Luke 9:31, the word translated as "departure" is *exodus*; the word translated as "accomplish" would be better translated as *complete*. Jesus' ministry was a "rescue event" which rescued humanity from the dominion of the deadly trio of Satan, sin, and death.

Lower section

THEREFORE

This section depicts the desired human response. God wants people to *serve one another in community* (***circle of small circles***, ***two servant figures***).

Since the fall into sin, human nature wants to reverse God's order of divine action (***BECAUSE***) and human response (***THEREFORE***). People think, "*Because* I am doing all these good things for God, *therefore* God will do good things for me." They see the commandments as a *merit system* (*a means of earning God's favor*) rather than as a *response system* (*guidelines for saying "thank you" to God for His mercy and goodness*).

FRAME 3

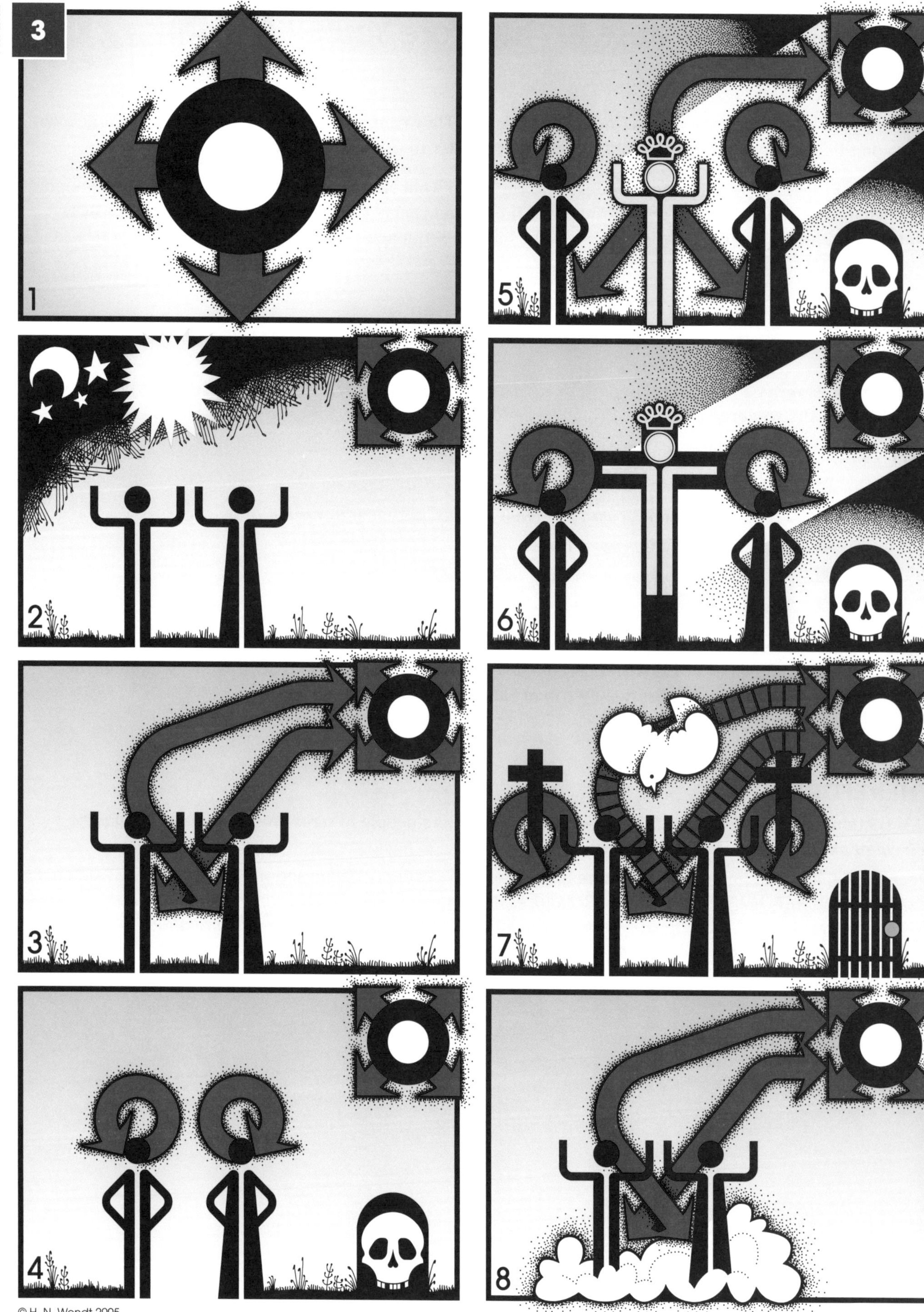

FRAME 3: The Divine Plan

The numbers below relate to the numbered sections in **ILLUSTRATION FRAME 3** (on the back of the time-line) .

1 "In the beginning, God..." Genesis 1:1 (***symbol for God***).

2 "created the heavens and the earth," Genesis 1:1 (***sun, moon, and stars***; ***surface of earth***). "Then God said, 'Let us make humankind,'" Genesis 1:26. "Male and female He created them," Genesis 1:27 (***male and female figures***).

3 "in our image, after our likeness," Genesis 1:26 (***people serve God and one another with out-going love***).

4 Humanity sinned (***people live to serve themselves***; ***note the break in the ground between the figures***). Death is the consequence (***tombstone with skull***), Romans 5:12, 6:23.

5 *People* changed. *God* did not. God became human in ***Jesus***, and ***lived for us the life we were meant to live***, but cannot.

6 ***Jesus suffered the death we deserve to die***. He did it *for us*. We do not have to die as punishment for sin any more, Galatians 4:4,5.

7 Jesus lived a sinless life for us, died to suffer the punishment we deserve, and rose again from the grave as Lord over death and eternity. He is among us through His Holy Spirit (***dove***).

a. He assures us that our sins are forgiven (***cross through sin***).
b. Death is transformed into a doorway leading to God's Eternal Home (***door with slats***). We can "see" in faith what lies on the other side of death.
c. Now we are to live as God first intended us to live (***arrows to God and neighbor***). The lines forming the arrows are ***broken***, because our obedience is, at best, imperfect.

8 In the life to come (the ***cloud*** symbolizes God's presence), God will restore things to the way He first intended them to be. In eternity, we shall perfectly ***praise God and serve others***.

FRAME
4
1
2
3
4
5
6
7
8
9
10
11
12
13
14
15

FRAME 4: Jesus, the Final Word of God

ILLUSTRATION FRAME 4 (on the back of the time-line) shows how all Old Testament themes must now be funneled (***funnel***) through the mind of Jesus the Messiah—the final interpreter of all Scriptures. On the funnel are symbols of ***Servant-King Jesus carrying His cross***, *Jesus' resurrection* (**open tomb**), and the *Holy Spirit* (***dove***). Jesus taught and showed His followers what His Father's heart was like, John 14:9 (***symbol for God***). The numbers below correspond to those in the illustration.

1 ***People:*** Our relationship with God is not established by ancestry, but by faith in Jesus as Savior and Lord, John 3:1–16; 14:6.

2 ***Land:*** The Christian hope centers around the life to come, not the land of Canaan, 1 Peter 1:3–5.

3 ***Rescue:*** Jesus rescues God's people, not from Egypt or Babylon, but from the powers of sin and death, Romans 6:20–23.

4 ***Sinai, covenant, law-code:*** Jesus is the presence of God among humanity, John 1:14. Jesus established the New Covenant (Mark 14:22–25), and Jesus alone determines how His followers are to live, Matthew 11:29,30.

5 ***False gods:*** Swiss theologian John Calvin said that the human mind is an idol factory. Martin Luther said that our "god" is whatever we devote life to. Anything that sidetracks us from living to serve God and others is idolatry, Ephesians 5:5.

6 ***Ark of the Covenant, sword:*** Jesus is the link between heaven and earth, John 1:51. Jesus calls and empowers us to fight the real enemy, Ephesians 6:10–18.

7 ***Crown:*** Jesus, the final descendant of David, is the eternal King of the universe, Hebrews 1:8.

8 ***Jerusalem:*** Christians look forward to entering the Eternal Jerusalem, Revelation 21:9–21.

9 ***Temple:*** God's Temple now consists of "living stones"—people joined by grace through faith to Jesus, 1 Peter 2:5; Ephesians 2:19–22.

10 ***Altar of sacrifice:*** God wants us to give Him our living bodies, to be used to His glory in the service of others, Romans 12:1.

11 ***Lamp*** (*Wisdom*), ***scroll:*** Jesus is the wisdom of God (1 Corinthians 1:24), and the Word of God, Hebrews 1:1,2. In Jesus, one greater than Solomon has come, Matthew 12:42.

12 ***Rule over the nations:*** In the latter part of the Old Testament period, some Jews hoped the day would come when they would rule the nations. In Daniel 7:11–14, the "son of man" (RSV) is a term for the Jewish people. However, Jesus is Lord of the nations, Ephesians 1:15–23.

13 ***Death and the grave:*** Jesus has overcome death and the power of the grave, and will one day command the realm of the dead to yield up the dead, John 5:25–29; 1 Corinthians 15.

14 ***Praying hands:*** Although the Old Testament contains many examples of prayer, Jesus' brothers and sisters look to Him for guidance in prayer, and as the model for prayer.

15 ***Funnel, Servant-King Jesus carrying His cross, open tomb, dove:*** Jesus the Messiah is Lord of Time and Eternity. **Jesus alone determines what Christians are to believe and how they are to live. Jesus is the model for the godly life.** We must direct all our questions to Jesus to obtain God's "final word," God's "final opinion," concerning what we are to believe and how we are to live.

FRAME 5

FRAME 5: Jesus, Master and Model

ILLUSTRATION FRAME 5 (on the back of the time-line). The New Testament teaches that the *Word of God* (***Bible***, *center*) that created the universe and directs the course of history became incarnate (*in-flesh*) in Jesus (***Servant-King***). God's people now look to Jesus for God's final Word concerning salvation and discipleship. The Christian faith is not *the most important part of life*; it is *life itself.* Christians are to see all of life as a sacred affair, lived around the presence of Jesus the Messiah. Their one desire is to reflect Jesus in all they do. How does this manifest itself in practical terms?

1 *Government* (***dome***): Christians take an active interest in, and serve in, government so as to enable all to live together harmoniously and happily at local, national, and international levels.

2 *Education* (***diplomas***): Christians develop their minds and abilities to be equipped to serve others in a meaningful, useful way.

3 *Food and drink* (***plate, knife and fork***): Christians eat healthfully in order to live usefully. They eat to live; they do not live to eat.

4 *Family life* (***parents with children***): The family is the basic unit of society. Parents influence children enormously—whether they realize it or not. The Christian faith must be taught, shared, modeled, and passed on in homes by parents who equip themselves to do so.

5 *The use of money* (***dollar sign***): Money is service in a storable, transferable form. It is not wrong to have money. The question is: How was it obtained, and how is it being used?

6 *Sport and leisure activities* (***ball***): People need to exercise and participate in healthy physical activities and leisure pursuits in order to keep their bodies and minds healthy and alert, that they may be better able to serve.

7 *Work* (***factory***): Christians see daily work as an opportunity to provide needed goods and services for the good of humanity.

8 *The organized church* (***church building***): According to the New Testament, the term "church" has to do with a community of people—never a building. Nevertheless, Christians gather with other Christians in an "ecclesiastical facility" to worship God together, to help one another grow in faith and discipleship, and to gather others into Jesus' community.

Kingdoms Come and Go

The *Secular* Story Behind the *Biblical* Story

When you take a Bible into your hands, you hold a priceless gift from God to humanity. The Bible reveals God's heart and God's plan for the cosmos and humanity for time and eternity. It is, above all, the inspired record of God's dialogue with humanity. This inspired conversation did not take place while the original participants were sitting in comfortable chairs. It took place within the turmoil of history.

Although the dialogue relates to all creation and history, it took place within a rather tiny corner of the world—the region known today as the Middle East. Most of it took place within that land variously called Canaan, Israel, Palestine, and the Holy Land.

Israel stands at the eastern end of the Mediterranean Sea. Still today, Israel's location is important politically and geographically. In the world in which the biblical narrative unfolds, Israel's history was greatly affected by the power play that went on among its neighbors to the south, north, east, and west.

The biblical writers wrote the events that constitute the biblical narrative while wearing "theological spectacles," so to say. What follows is a condensed account of how a secular historian might have reported the events behind the Old Testament narrative.

1 The Big Political Players: A Summary

The ancient nation of Israel stood where three continents meet—Africa, Asia, and Europe. To the south of Israel, in Africa, lies Egypt. When the biblical story begins, Egypt is already an old empire. As a succession of dynasties came and went, Egypt's political power and influence rose and fell.

Recent events in the world have made people today more familiar with names such as Syria, Iraq, and Iran. These countries are located within or near the valleys of the Tigris and Euphrates Rivers—a region traditionally referred to as "Mesopotamia." Mesopotamia is made up of two Greek words for "between the rivers." In biblical times, this region was controlled by a succession of empires: the Assyrian, Babylonian, and Medo-Persian empires.

Later, and to the west, came the Greek and Roman empires. First, Alexander the Great and his successors conquered and controlled the eastern Mediterranean region, and sought to impose Greek philosophy and culture on all they controlled. Later, the Romans swallowed up the Greek empire, took control of all regions around the Mediterranean rim, and expanded their empire to dominate the regions west of Rome.

2 Closer Neighbors and Troublemakers

The Israelites who entered Canaan after the Exodus from Egypt had to determine what to do with that land's original inhabitants, the Canaanites. They also had to deal with the Philistines, who settled along the Mediterranean coast, and controlled the five cities of Gath, Gaza, Ashkelon, Ashdod, and Ekron. They had to deal with the Arameans (Syrians), whose capital city was Damascus. And they had to deal with other lesser tribes and kingdoms located around their borders, namely, the Ammonites, Moabites, Edomites, Ishmaelites, Midianites and Amalekites—most of whom were related to them.

3 The Egyptian Connection

During the period 1550–1200 B.C., Egypt claimed control over Syria and Palestine. However, Egypt's claims were often contested by the Hittites and the Mitanni peoples of eastern Asia Minor. By 1200 B.C., Egyptian control of Palestine was more theory than fact, and numerous groups from within and without

Palestine were fighting to control various parts of it. The resulting instability took its toll on the region's trade and economy. The Amarna letters, written during the reigns of the Egyptian pharaohs Amenhotep III and IV (ca. 1403–1347 B.C.), allude to the events of this period.

The book of Exodus describes God's rescue of Jacob's descendants from Egypt as the key event in their history. The Israelites continued to remember Egypt as the land of bondage from which God rescued them with "signs and wonders," Deuteronomy 26:8. Centuries later, a small group of fugitives from Judah, fearing Babylonian wrath, fled back to Egypt—taking the prophet Jeremiah with them, Jeremiah chs. 42–44. This was demoralizing; to return to Egypt was to undo the Exodus!

In the Land

The book of Joshua describes the Israelite conquest of Canaan. The book of Judges describes, among other things, the three major problems the new residents in Palestine faced: political disunity, spiritual syncretism (a mixing of religious beliefs and practices), and dynastic uncertainty. The opening chapters of 1 Samuel describe how the Israelites eventually came to have kings—the first of whom was Saul. However, by the time of Saul's death, the Philistines and the Ammonites seemed to control much of the land. The writer of 1 Samuel 13:19–22 states that the Israelites had to look to the Philistines to supply them with weapons of war and tools for agriculture.

Indications are that King David (Saul's successor) managed to deal with the Philistine threat. Under David and his successor, Solomon, Israel became the dominant power in the region and experienced its golden age. But when Solomon died, the previously United Kingdom split into two small kingdoms: Israel to the north and Judah to the south.

To complicate matters, about five years after Solomon's death, Pharaoh Shishak I of Egypt sought to reassert Egyptian control over the regions to his north, and plundered Israel and Judah, Jerusalem, and its Temple, 1 Kings 14:25–28. However, the Egyptians were not able to maintain tight control over Judah and Israel, and played only a sporadic role in the power struggles of the next several centuries.

As Egyptian power waned, nations to the north, east, and west of Israel continued to cast covetous eyes on Egypt. Little wonder, because Egypt, with its remarkably fertile and productive Nile Valley, was the breadbasket of the ancient world. However, nations such as those in Mesopotamia could not travel "as the crow flies" to Egypt because of the deserts in between. Travel across desert regions became possible only with the domestication of the camel, and even then, no nation could provide every member of its army with a personal "ship of the desert." Armies traveled by foot. So, as nation after nation strove to gain control of Egypt, they marched through—and annexed—Israel, for Israel lay on the land-bridge between Egypt to the south and Egypt's covetous competitors to the north.

Syria and Phoenicia: Squabbles and Alliances

Israel and Judah's close neighbors, Syria and Phoenicia, were also subject to threats from the armies of powerful empires. Yet these nations squabbled among themselves as well. The Old Testament tells us that Israel, Syria, and Phoenicia were each striving to become the dominant force in the region. Commerce and control of trade routes were motivating forces. It was to Phoenicia's benefit to try to maintain good relations with Israel and Syria. Phoenicia's economy was based on seafaring trade among Mediterranean nations, and its traders needed goods produced by Israel and Syria. Furthermore, goods from more distant countries had to pass through Israel and Syria to reach Phoenician ships.

Some of the rulers of Phoenicia, Syria, and Israel used treaties and marriages to forge political alliances. For example, during the reigns of Omri of Israel, and his successor and son Ahab, relations between Israel and Syria were strained. At the same time, relations between Israel and Phoenicia were good, and were sealed by the marriage of Jezebel, the daughter of the king of the Phoenician city of Sidon, and Ahab, king of Israel, 1 Kings 16:31. This, in turn, led to something of a marriage between Phoenicia and Israel's cultural and religious traditions. It also gave the affluent in Israel access to Phoenician luxuries such as ivory furnishings, Amos 6:4. (Jerusalem, Judah's capital, reflected Phoenician influence, too; its Temple was designed by Phoenician architects using a Phoenician pattern, 1 Kings 5.)

Assyria

With the gradual weakening of Egyptian influence, the Neo-Assyrian Empire in Mesopotamia increased in power and influence, and soon became an influential presence in the histories of Israel and Judah, and those of other regions between Assyria and Egypt, such as Syria and Phoenicia. To deal with the threat, several states in the region of Syria and Israel joined forces in an effort to stem the Assyrian advance into their territory. In 853 B.C., the opposing sides locked horns at Qarqar. King Ahab of Israel was said to have sent 2,000 chariots and 10,000 foot soldiers to battle. The coalition of smaller states came out the apparent winner over Assyria. However, because necessity had been the mother of cooperation in the battle of Qarqar, relations among these small states remained uneasy.

Although Judah took no part in the encounter at Qarqar, it could not isolate itself entirely from foreign influence and the power struggles that were taking place in the region. Judah sought to pursue a policy of isolationism, but such a policy was impossible. In 735 B.C., Syria and Israel joined forces in an attempt to force Ahaz of Judah to join them in a military venture designed to stem Assyrian incursions into the area.

In seeking to secure itself within Mesopotamia, Assyria set out to establish buffer regions around its borders, and to control Egypt to obtain a sure source of food for its armies. In 721 B.C., Assyria swallowed up Israel and led its people into exile and oblivion. Judah was made a vassal of Assyria, and was forced to pay an annual tribute and to support Assyrian military ventures in the region.

Egypt, being well aware of Assyria's ambitions, set out to make the small states to its immediate north a buffer between itself and Assyria. To achieve its goal, Egypt made numerous promises to those small northern neighbors, but rarely kept them. Isaiah referred to Egypt as a broken cane that offered little support to those who leaned on it; Egypt was, in fact, dangerous, Isaiah 36:6.

While all this was going on, prophets such as Amos, Hosea, Isaiah, and Micah watched, thought, and taught. Although politically they sensed what Assyrian ambitions would eventually mean for Israel and Judah, what they said and wrote went beyond political opinion to spiritual diagnosis. They interpreted what they saw in theological terms. They understood clearly that there is no such thing as a purely secular event.

Babylon

Although Assyria gained control of Egypt in the middle of the 7th century B.C., Assyria overextended itself in doing so, found it could not maintain its military machine, and finally lost its grip on Egypt, 2 Kings 23:29–35. With Assyria's demise, another player walked on to the stage of history—Babylon! Egypt immediately saw the emerging Babylon as a threat, with the result that, in 609 B.C., Pharaoh Neco of Egypt led his armies north in an attempt to prop up a dying Assyria. Although Neco's efforts were short-lived and unsuccessful, they drastically changed the history of Judah. Because Judah felt it

had suffered long enough under the Assyrian heel, more than anything else Judah wanted Babylon to deliver the final thrust to a dying Assyria. Therefore, King Josiah of Judah, in an effort to stem Neco's advance, led his army into battle against the Egyptians. In the ensuing battle at Megiddo, the Egyptians proved the victors, and Josiah lost his life, 2 Kings 23:28–30.

The kings of Judah who succeeded Josiah (two sons, a grandson, and then another son) sought to secure their throne and borders by playing off one neighboring power against the other. They failed, and brought about the collapse of Judah in the process. After King Jehoiakim (Josiah's son) revolted in 601 B.C., King Nebuchadnezzar of Babylon marched around the Fertile Crescent and put the revolt down. Jehoiakim died three months before Jerusalem's fall in 597 B.C. His son Jehoiachin, who replaced him, surrendered immediately, and, together with thousands of others, was taken into exile in Babylon. Another son of Josiah, Zedekiah, was made a puppet king, replacing Jehoiachin. When he, too, revolted in 589 B.C., Nebuchadnezzar stormed around the Fertile Crescent, devastated Judah, sacked and destroyed Jerusalem and its Temple, killed many of its political and religious leaders (including Zedekiah's sons), and again took thousands into exile, including Zedekiah whom he had blinded.

The Babylonians, like the Assyrians before them, set out to control subject peoples through fear, and destroy national identities and religious allegiances by removing those they conquered from their nation-state, and assimilating them with other captive ethnic groups.

In the ancient biblical world, many believed that when a nation died, its deity had died—or was showing impotence or lack of concern for its people. In contrast, many who experienced the exile in Babylon came to understand that their God was not confined to any particular territory, nor was their God limited in power. There were other ways of explaining their presence as exiles in Babylon. And so, although Psalm 137:4 contains the cry of a people recently removed from their national state and national shrine, many came to see that they could worship and serve God even while living in lands other than Judah. This learning process was made easier by the overthrow of Babylon by Cyrus the Persian in 539 B.C.

8 Enter Persia

In 539 B.C., Babylonian power gave way to Persian power when Cyrus the Persian and his successors carved out a kingdom that stretched from India to Ethiopia. Cyrus saw his capture of Babylon as a grant of Marduk, the chief god of Babylon, who declared him the legitimate king of the city. The city had, in fact, been handed over to Cyrus by Babylonian priests who were disenchanted with Nabonidus, the last of the Babylonian kings. The priests were angered since Nabonidus had deserted Babylon to reside in northwest Arabia. In addition, he made his son, Belshazzar, regent in Babylon, and for ten years, he had not attended the annual New Year Festival for the enthronement of Marduk in Babylon. Even Isaiah spoke of Cyrus as God's "messiah," 44:28–45:1.

Cyrus pursued an enlightened policy. He permitted foreign exiles within his realm to return to their homelands and to reestablish their religious practices—as long as the move did not interfere with the peace and stability of the empire. However, although many exiles returned to Judah, they were not permitted to establish themselves as an independent nation, but remained part of the Persian *satrapy* (province) known as "Beyond the River."

Those who returned to Judah became known as "Jews," and developed the system of belief that still today is known as "Judaism." Although they were grateful for the rights and privileges they enjoyed under the Persians, they experienced some agony. King Jehoiachin, who had been taken to Babylon in 597 B.C., was still alive in 560 B.C., 2 Kings 25:27–30. Many hoped that when the period of exile in

Babylon ended, Jehoiachin would return to Jerusalem with them to reestablish the Davidic dynasty and kingdom. Their hopes were not fulfilled; Jehoiachin did not live long enough to join the exiles who returned to Judah. He died in Babylon some time after 560 B.C. The result was that those who eventually returned to reestablish themselves in Judah and Jerusalem felt that, although God had rescued them from Babylon, two things were wrong.

- *First*, they remained under foreign control.
- *Second*, the Davidic dynasty had apparently come to an end.

Despite these frustrations, for several hundred years the Jews enjoyed a period of peace and stability they had not known for centuries.

Although many of the exiles continued to live beyond the borders of Judah, with many rising to high rank—Esther and Mordecai, for example—many others deliberately developed a lifestyle that would set them apart from those non-Jews among whom they lived. Increasing importance was placed on Sabbath observances, circumcision, food laws, and Passover observance within the family context.

Enter Greece

During the Persian period, the Jews had been able to preserve their religious identity without too much difficulty. But in 331 B.C., the Persian Empire fell to that of Alexander the Great of Macedon. Alexander was 20 years old when he came to power; his father had been assassinated. With the advent of Greek control, Alexander and his successors sought to impose Hellenism (Greek philosophy, language, and way of life) on all within the borders of their empire.

Upon Alexander's death in 323 B.C., the Greek Empire was divided into three parts. One general, Ptolemy, gained control of Egypt. A second general, Seleucus, ruled the Mesopotamian region and, for a time, his territories extended to the borders of India. A third section, extending around Greece itself, was torn by wars of succession until the Romans assumed control of the region in the second century B.C.

To complicate matters, Judah found itself caught up in a tug-of-war between the Ptolemies who ruled Egypt, and the Seleucids who ruled both Syria and the territories to the east. The Ptolemies eventually managed to gain control over Judah, and retained that control until 198 B.C. when the Seleucids took over.

Although the returning exiles had rebuilt the Jerusalem Temple and rededicated it in 515 B.C., and although Jews scattered beyond the borders of Judah (*diaspora* Jews) felt a strong attachment to that sacred edifice, few of them could visit it. Furthermore, although many *diaspora* Jews supported the financial needs of the Temple, the family circle and the synagogue served as the focal points for community life in the regions beyond Judah's borders.

Although the Greeks did not at first use force to impose Hellenism on subject peoples, they let it be known that their traditions and way of life were superior. The temples, gymnasiums, and theaters they built appealed strongly to many among their subject peoples, including some of the more youthful Jews and the Jewish upper class. Many Jews learned to speak Greek. The time came when many Jews could speak *only* Greek—with the result that during the last centuries B.C., the Jews in Alexandria translated their sacred writings into Greek. They added several other Greek texts (today referred to as the *Apocrypha*) to the Hebrew texts they translated. The final collection became known as the *Septuagint*.

Kingdoms Come and Go (continued)

As time went by, an increasing number of Jews adopted Greek dress and customs, took part in Greek games, and studied Greek philosophy. They blended Judaism and Hellenism and ignored Jewish dietary requirements. Aspiring Jewish male athletes sought to have the marks of circumcision reversed surgically. Some applauded these moves. Others were appalled by them.

In 168 B.C., the Seleucid ruler, Antiochus IV "Epiphanes", set out to eliminate Judaism completely and replace it with Hellenism. He sought to do away with Sabbath observance, circumcision, dietary practices, and the possession of the Torah. To cap it all off, he tried to enforce the worship of Greek gods—and even of himself as the incarnation of the deity. Some Jews readily conformed to his dictates. Others conformed merely to save their lives. Some withdrew into hiding to practice their Jewish ways. Others suffered martyrdom, 2 Maccabees chs. 6,7.

The breaking point came when Antiochus ordered Jews to offer pagan sacrifices. In 167 B.C., some Jews under the leadership of the Maccabees (a Jewish priestly family) revolted—and managed to remove the Seleucid yoke from their necks. Although Antiochus had desecrated the Temple in 168 B.C., the Maccabees purified and rededicated it in 165 B.C.—an event which the Jews continue to celebrate annually at Hanukkah. Then, from about 165 to 63 B.C., the Jews enjoyed a measure of political freedom under the rule, first of the Maccabees, and then of their descendants and successors, the Hasmoneans.

Even so, all was not well within the realm. First, the Seleucids had been ready to strike a deal with the Maccabees because they were aware of the growing might of Rome. Second, the Jews soon realized that although they had won the war against the Seleucids, they had lost the peace—for the Hasmoneans who ruled them did so more in the manner of Greek princes than Jewish leaders.

10 **Finally, Rome**

During the first century B.C., Rome began to make its presence felt more and more around the Mediterranean basin. In 63 B.C., the Roman general Pompey took control of Judea (a postexilic Roman term for Judah). The Romans took advantage of a bitter rivalry between two Hasmoneans, Hyrcanus II, who had succeeded to the throne in 67 B.C., and his brother, the vicious Aristobulus. The Romans chose the weaker brother, Hyrcanus, as their representative; Pompey named him High Priest.

Hyrcanus' chief minister was his close friend, Antipater, from the province of Idumea, the Roman name for the territory of Edom. Antipater was politically shrewd. He earned gratitude from Julius Caesar for his loyalty. Among his rewards were powerful positions for his sons, Herod and Phasael. Herod, too, proved his loyalty to Rome, and was nominated by the Roman senate to be king of Judea in 40 B.C. He was not able to succeed to his position until 37 B.C. since the Parthians had invaded and claimed Judea in the meantime; Herod had to reconquer the territory with Roman help.

After Herod's death in 4 B.C., the Romans appointed his son Archelaeus as ethnarch ("ruler of the people") of Judea and Samaria, but deposed him in A.D. 6. After that time, except for one brief period, Judea was governed by Roman officials known as prefects and procurators, few of whom were sensitive enough to govern the unique people they were sent to rule. The name of one of those procurators remains prominent in history: Pontius Pilate.

In Matthew 2:1, we read, "In the time of King Herod, after Jesus was born in Bethlehem of Judah..."
In Matthew 27:26, we read, "After flogging Jesus, Pilate handed him over to be crucified."

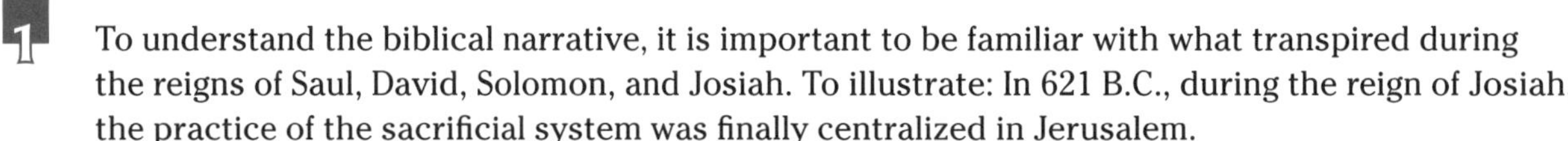

From Saul to Josiah

Key Old Testament Narratives: Saul, David, Solomon, and Josiah

Preliminary Comments

1 To understand the biblical narrative, it is important to be familiar with what transpired during the reigns of Saul, David, Solomon, and Josiah. To illustrate: In 621 B.C., during the reign of Josiah, the practice of the sacrificial system was finally centralized in Jerusalem.

2 There is reason to believe that the narrative outlining Israelite history (Joshua, Judges, Samuel, and Kings) was completed in Babylon after 560 B.C., 2 Kings 25:27–30.

3 It is possible that an *earlier* edition of the narrative was completed during the reign of Josiah, 2 Kings 23:25. This earlier edition reflects optimism, for it presents Josiah as the one who restored the Davidic Kingdom. After all, Josiah, a descendant of David, ruled Judah—and eventually Israel—from Jerusalem, and made the Jerusalem Temple the focal point of the nation's worship life, and the only legitimate place for offering sacrifice, 2 Kings chs. 22,23.

4 The *later* edition, completed some time after 560 B.C., grieves over the fact that the people of God are in exile in Babylon. It struggles with questions such as: "Why are we here? Where did we go wrong? Will we ever go back to Judah and Jerusalem? Will the Davidic dynasty ever be restored?" It finds hope in the fact that Jehoiachin, taken to Babylon in 597 B.C. at the age of 18, is still alive in 560 B.C., and because he is 55 years of age, there is a chance that he might live through the exile, return to Jerusalem, and restore the Davidic dynasty.

5 In the Old Testament, the spirit of God raises up, and/or comes upon, the judges Othniel, Gideon, Jephthah, and Samson, then King Saul (1 Samuel 10:6–13; 19:23,24) and King David, 1 Samuel 16:13; note 16:14,15. After David, the next king upon whom the spirit of God comes is Jesus the Messiah. However, during the intervening period, the spirit of God comes upon the prophets—who tell the kings they are to live under God's covenant and rule according to it.

Prior to Saul

1 The central theme of 1 Samuel 1:1–7:2 is how the Ark of the Covenant got from the shrine at Shiloh (in Ephraim) to Kiriath-jearim. Along the way, the presence of the Ark caused considerable discomfort to the Philistines—who had captured it from Israel. The Philistines sent it back from their land to the Holy Land on a wagon hauled by cows. Some years later, David retrieved it from Kiriath-jearim and placed it in a special tent he built for it in Jerusalem, 2 Samuel 6; note especially verse 17. The nature of the shrine in Shiloh is uncertain, 1 Samuel 1:9,24; 2:22; 3:3,15. Although the Ark of the Covenant was deposited in Kiriath-jearim (1 Samuel 7:2), it turned up in other locations during Samuel's time (1 Samuel 10:17), and also during Saul's reign, 1 Samuel 14:18; 21:1–6. See also Judges 20:26–28.

2 1 Samuel chs. 1-3 tell about the birth of Samuel (a Levite according to 1 Chronicles 6:33ff), and the deaths of Eli and his sons–the priests who cared for the shrine at Shiloh. Later, Abiathar–a priest who had served at Shiloh and who managed to escape when Saul killed all priests serving at that shrine--was accepted into David's inner circle, 1 Samuel chs. 21,22. However, eventually, Solomon banished Abiathar (who had supported Adonijah's bid for David's throne, 1 Kings 1:5-7), and the priest Zadok rose to prominence and power in Solomon's court, 1 Kings 1;8, 32-40.

3 Both Eli's sons (1 Samuel 2:12–17, 22) and Samuel's sons (1 Samuel 8:1–3) were viewed as unfit to succeed their respective fathers in office. Hence, the issues that needed to be determined were those of succession and the form of government. Finally, Saul was appointed king, 1 Samuel chs. 8–11.

4 The appointment of a ruler is outlined in 1 Samuel chs. 8–12. The terms "king" and "prince" (RSV translation) weave their way through the narratives in these chapters. The term prince is always positive, for God is still seen as king of the people and the prince as merely God's earthly representative. The term *king* can be viewed in a good sense, but whenever the future ruler is thought of negatively, the term king (not prince) is used. Solomon appears to be the villain in 1 Samuel 8:10–18.

Saul (1 Samuel)

1 In 1 Samuel chs. 8–11, Saul himself is never referred to negatively. However, Samuel deposed Saul from office on two occasions. Why? In ch. 13, Saul performed a ritual that only a priest should have performed (see 10:8) and, in ch. 15, he failed to kill all of Israel's enemies in a "holy war."

2 The term "a man after God's own heart" first appears in 1 Samuel 13:14. The narrative that follows reveals that the term implies, "David worshiped one God in one place—Jerusalem."

3 In ch. 14, although Saul's son Jonathan displays skill as a soldier in battle, no reference is made to him consulting or praying to God prior to fighting the Philistines. Perhaps the suggestion is that David is a more appropriate candidate to succeed Saul.

4 In 1 Samuel 16, David is enlisted into Saul's service as a musician and armor-bearer.

5 First Samuel tells several other stories about how David first entered Saul's service, 17:17ff, 17:31ff, 17:55ff. Although 1 Samuel 17 states that David killed Goliath, 2 Samuel 21:19 ascribes the achievement to Elhanan (but see also 1 Chronicles 20:5).

6 In 1 Samuel 18:1–4, Jonathan gives David tokens suggesting he knows (and accepts!) that David will be the next king.

7 Saul tries to pin David to the wall with a spear, 18:10,11.

8 Saul gives David his *second* daughter (Michal) in marriage, rather than (as promised) his *first* daughter, Merab, 18:17–29.

9 In 1 Samuel 19, David and Jonathan have the first of a series of amicable conversations.

10 Saul tries to pin David to the wall with a spear a second time, 19:8–10.

11 David flees from Michal (and Saul), possibly on their wedding night, 19:11–17.

12 David flees to Ramah, and Saul pursues him, 19:18–24.

13 The spirit of God comes on Saul a second time, 19:23,24; see 10:6–13.

14 Jonathan talks to David, and Saul tries to kill Jonathan, ch. 20; note 20:14–17.

15 David gets food and Goliath's sword from the priests at Nob, ch. 21:1–9.

16 David tries to become a vassal of the Philistines, 21:10–15.

17 David gathers a band of supporters, 22:1,2.

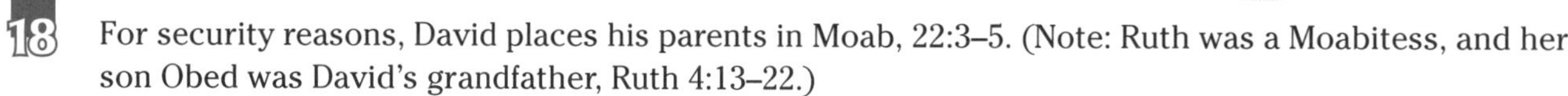

18 For security reasons, David places his parents in Moab, 22:3–5. (Note: Ruth was a Moabitess, and her son Obed was David's grandfather, Ruth 4:13–22.)

19 Saul kills the priests at Nob, 22:6–23.

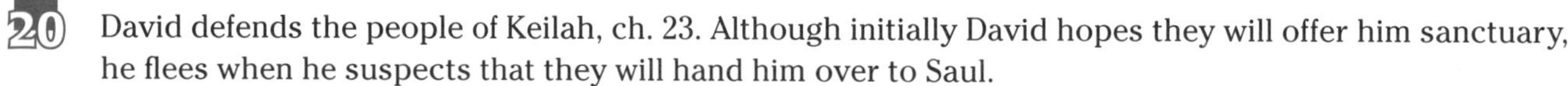

20 David defends the people of Keilah, ch. 23. Although initially David hopes they will offer him sanctuary, he flees when he suspects that they will hand him over to Saul.

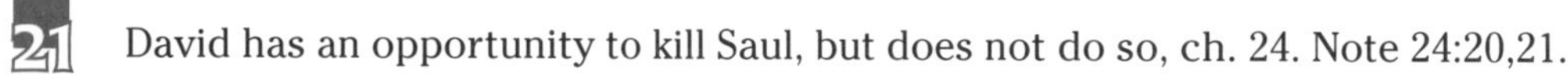

21 David has an opportunity to kill Saul, but does not do so, ch. 24. Note 24:20,21.

22 David runs a "protection business," ch. 25.

23 David gets some new wives (Abigail and *Ahinoam*), and Saul gives his daughter, Michal, to another man, 25:39–44. According to 1 Samuel 14:50, Saul was married to a woman named *Ahinoam*.

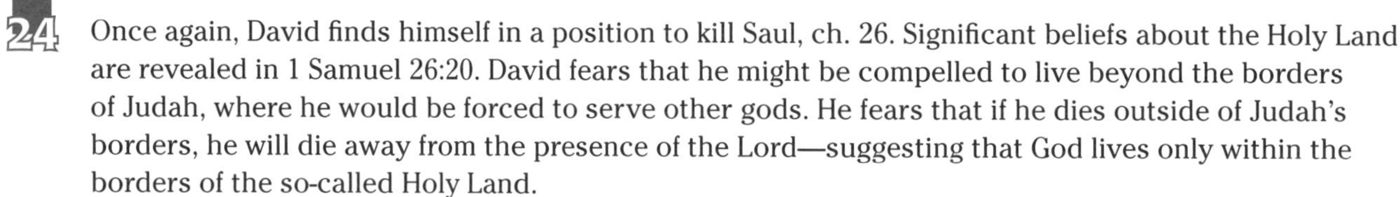

24 Once again, David finds himself in a position to kill Saul, ch. 26. Significant beliefs about the Holy Land are revealed in 1 Samuel 26:20. David fears that he might be compelled to live beyond the borders of Judah, where he would be forced to serve other gods. He fears that if he dies outside of Judah's borders, he will die away from the presence of the Lord—suggesting that God lives only within the borders of the so-called Holy Land.

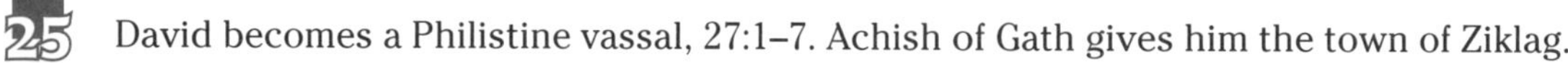

25 David becomes a Philistine vassal, 27:1–7. Achish of Gath gives him the town of Ziklag.

26 David annihilates the Amalekites, and lies to the Philistines, 27:8–12.

27 Saul consults the witch at Endor, ch. 28. She predicts Saul's approaching death.

28 Note the tension: Will David be forced to fight against his own people, ch. 29? After David is "off the hook," he returns to Ziklag to find it plundered, ch. 30. When David's followers contemplate killing him, he redeems himself by recovering all the lost spoils taken by the Amalekites, 30:6.

29 David sends presents to the clan leaders of Judah, 30:26–31. It is, after all, "election year," and Saul is about to lose his life.

30 Saul and his army are defeated at the battle of Gilboa. Three of Saul's sons are killed, including Jonathan, 31:2. Saul commits suicide, and is eventually buried by the men of Jabesh-gilead, 31:4,11–13. (Note: For background on Jabesh-gilead, see Judges 19–21 and 1 Samuel 11; also 2 Samuel 2:4b–7. Furthermore, 1 Chronicles 10:6 states that the Philistines wiped out Saul's entire family, thus saving David the task of having to do so, 2 Samuel 21.)

David

Jonathan had extracted from David the promise that, when David became king, he would not annihilate Jonathan's family, 1 Samuel 20:12–17. David made a similar promise to Saul, 1 Samuel 24:16–22. Abigail eventually vindicated what David did to his opponents, 1 Samuel 25:23–31, especially vv. 29–31.

In fitting together the Saul/David narrative, it is helpful to remember that Abner, Saul's general, was Saul's cousin, 1 Samuel 14:50. Joab, David's general, was David's nephew and Solomon's cousin, as was also Amasa whom David's son Absalom chose to be his general; see 2 Samuel 17:25, and note that Zeruiah was David's sister. Joab eventually killed both Abner and Amasa, and on his deathbed David instructed Solomon to have Joab put to death, 1 Kings 2:1–9.

From Saul to Josiah (continued)

1 After lamenting for Saul and Jonathan (2 Samuel ch. 1), David is made king of Judah at Hebron, 2:1–4a.

2 The Northern Kingdom does not want David for its king, 2:4b–7. Abner, Saul's cousin and general, makes Saul's son, Ishbosheth, king of the North, 2:8–11.

3 A brutal contest is staged between representatives of Israel and Judah, 2:12–32. Eventually, Abner kills Asahel, David's nephew and a brother of Joab (David's general, and also his nephew). There now erupts a long war between Judah and Israel , 3:1.

4 David obtains more wives and concubines in *Hebron*, 3:2–5. They bear him six sons.

5 Abner apparently tries to make himself king of the northern part of the Promised Land, 3:6–11, but fails in the attempt. He schemes with David to have David gain control of the North, 3:12–21.

6 Joab kills Abner. After all, if there is to be one realm, there is room for only one general, 3:22–39. The northern king is beheaded; David has his executioners brutally killed, ch. 4.

7 David gains control over the northern realm as well as over Judah, 5:1–5.

8 David captures Jerusalem, 5:6–10. He has the city's blind and lame killed, and forbids them entry into the Temple that Solomon, his son, will eventually build (see Matthew 21:14).

9 David builds himself a palace, 5:11,12.

10 David obtains more wives and concubines in *Jerusalem*, 5:13–16; note that Solomon was born in Jerusalem.

11 David subdues the Philistines, 5:17–25. They eventually serve as his bodyguards, 15:18.

12 David brings the Ark of the Covenant to Jerusalem, and puts it into a tent, ch. 6. David's first wife (Michal, Saul's daughter) is dismissed from his favor and bedroom. See 1 Samuel 18:20–27; 25:44; 2 Samuel 3:12–16; 6:16, 20–23.

13 David decides to build God a "house," or a Temple, ch. 7. God says He does not want a Temple, 7:4–7. God says, however, that He will make a "house," or a dynasty, out of David (7:8–17) that will last "forever," 7:13,16,29. David thanks God for the promise of a dynasty, but does not refer to any future Temple while doing so, 7:18–29.

14 David expands his kingdom—brutally, 2 Samuel chs. 8 and 10.

15 David "shows kindness" to Jonathan's son, Mephibosheth, ch. 9. It is possible that he placed him under house arrest. Some believe, with good reason, that ch. 9 should follow ch. 21.

16 David seduces Bathsheba, chs. 11,12. This action involved adultery, murder, and the breaking of holy war laws which said: "During war, *no sex*," Deuteronomy 20; 1 Samuel 21:4. The story Nathan, the prophet, tells David (2 Samuel 12:1–14) to trap him into admitting his guilt is based on the laws of restitution found in Exodus 22:1

17 David's son, Amnon, rapes his half-sister Tamar, 13:1–19.

18 Absalom, Amnon's half-brother and Tamar's full-brother, has Amnon killed, 13:20–33. Absalom flees to his maternal grandfather, Talmai, king of Geshur, 13:34–39.

19 Joab arranges for Absalom to return to Jerusalem—and to the family circle, ch. 14.

20 Absalom begins casting doubt on David's administrative ability, 15:1–6.

21 Absalom gets David's permission to visit Hebron, Absalom's place of birth and David's first capital. Absalom and his supporters cry "Revolt!" against David at Hebron, 15:7–11.

22 David's chief counselor, Ahithophel, joins Absalom in his plot against David, 15:12,13.

23 David hears about the revolt, and—with his bodyguard—flees from Jerusalem, 15:13–18. Although many of David's own people have rebelled against him, Ittai the Gittite (who is in charge of David's Philistine mercenaries) remains loyal to him, 15:19–23. David weeps as he leaves Jerusalem, 15:30; see Luke 19:41.

24 David sends Abiathar, Zadok, the Levites, and the Ark back to Jerusalem, 15:24–29.

25 David hears that Ahithophel has joined forces with Absalom, 15:31. He sends Hushai back to Jerusalem to serve as his spy in Absalom's court, 15:32–37. Ziba tells David that Jonathan's son, Mephibosheth, hopes to regain Saul's throne, 16:1–4. (Ziba is Mephibosheth's servant.) David later accepts Mephibosheth's denial of evil intent—but with some misgivings, 19:24–30.

26 Shimei, a Benjaminite, mocks David as he flees Jerusalem, 16:5–14. Although David's bodyguard wants to kill Shimei, David forbids it. David arrives at Mahanaim, Ishbosheth's former capital, 17:24–29.

27 When Absalom and his supporters enter Jerusalem, Hushai persuades them to let him join them, 16:15–19. Absalom had appointed Amasa, his cousin and David's nephew, to serve as his general, 17:24–26, 1 Chronicles 2:13–17.

28 Ahithophel advises Absalom to have sex with David's concubines, 16:20–23. By doing so, Absalom declares, "I have taken over David's harem—and therefore am now the king!"

29 Ahithophel comes up with the perfect plan to establish Absalom on the throne, 17:1–4. Hushai wrecks that plan, 17:5–22.

30 Knowing that David will defeat Absalom and kill him, Ahithophel commits suicide, 17:23. Ahithophel was Bathsheba's grandfather, 11:3, 23:34.

31 Joab kills Absalom in the Forest of Ephraim, ch. 18:1–18. David laments for his son, 18:19–33.

32 David strives to restore a divided and disorganized realm, 19:1–15. David, angry with Joab, appoints Amasa (Absalom's general) as his general (19:13)—a healing, reconciling gesture. David also assures Shimei (a Benjaminite, who cursed him) that he will not seek vengeance, 19:16–23.

33 Jonathan's son, Mephibosheth, assures David that he was not plotting to gain the throne, 19:24–30.

34 David places the ten concubines, with whom Absalom slept, into life-long seclusion, 20:3.

35 The Northern Kingdom, led by Sheba, breaks away from David, 20:1,2. Amasa, David's new general, is slow in quelling the revolt, 20:4,5. Abishai is now told to take control of the army. After Abishai tells his brother Joab what is taking place, Joab kills Amasa, regains control of the army, and crushes the revolt, 20:6–26.

From Saul to Josiah (continued)

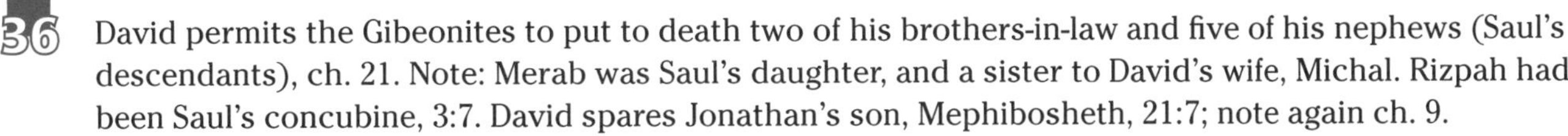

36 David permits the Gibeonites to put to death two of his brothers-in-law and five of his nephews (Saul's descendants), ch. 21. Note: Merab was Saul's daughter, and a sister to David's wife, Michal. Rizpah had been Saul's concubine, 3:7. David spares Jonathan's son, Mephibosheth, 21:7; note again ch. 9.

37 Chs. 22,23: Hymns of praise, and David's dealings with the Philistines.

38 David conducts a census, is disciplined, and buys the threshing floor of Araunah the Jebusite, the site upon which Solomon's Temple was eventually built, ch. 24.

David's Last Days and Words, and Death (1 Kings 1:1–2:9)

1 David is old—and cold, 1:1–4. Abishag, the most beautiful girl in Israel, is placed into David's bed to keep him warm—and to determine whether he is capable of having sex. Because he is apparently sexually impotent, David is no longer considered fit to be king.

2 David's son Adonijah assumes he will succeed his father, and makes arrangements for his own coronation, 1:5–10.

3 The prophet Nathan and David's wife Bathsheba persuade David to declare another son, Solomon, to be his successor, 1:11–31. David has Solomon anointed as king, 1:32–40.

4 Adonijah is terrified, and seeks refuge in the Jerusalem sanctuary, 1:41–53. Solomon places his brother under house arrest.

5 David, prior to his death, gives Solomon some final instructions:

   a. First, he instructs Solomon to be obedient to the Lord, to walk in His ways, and to keep His statutes, commandments, ordinances, and testimonies so that the Davidic dynasty might continue, 2:1–4. This means: Solomon is to offer sacrifice to the one God in only one place—the Jerusalem Temple!

   b. David then asks Solomon to kill Joab (David's nephew and general, and Solomon's cousin) and Shimei (who had mocked and cursed him), 2:5–9.

6 David's death is reported in the verses that immediately follow, 2:10–12.

Solomon

1 Adonijah, Solomon's brother, asks to be given David's last-assigned concubine, Abishag the Shunammite, as his wife. Solomon has Adonijah killed, 1 Kings 2:13–25.

2 Solomon sends the priest, Abiathar, into exile, 1 Kings 2:26–27. Abiathar had supported Adonijah in his bid for the throne, 1 Kings 1:5–8.

3 Solomon has Joab killed, 2:28–35.

4 Solomon has Shimei killed, 2:36–46.

5 Solomon is established as king, 2:46.

6 Reference is made to Solomon's building program, and his marriage to an Egyptian princess, 3:1.

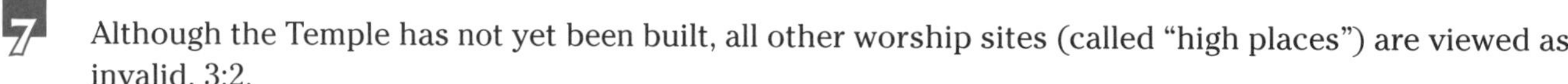

7 Although the Temple has not yet been built, all other worship sites (called "high places") are viewed as invalid, 3:2.

8 Solomon worships at shrines other than that in Jerusalem—according to the writers, a bad thing, 3:3. Although the Gibeon shrine is considered invalid, God appears to Solomon there, 3:4,5. Note the references to David's "faithfulness, righteousness, uprightness," 3:6, 11:4,6. These imply: David worshiped one God in Jerusalem.

9 Solomon prays for wisdom, 3:7–14. Compare 3:11 with 2:25,34,46, and note how Solomon did not need to ask for the death of his enemies—he has already had them killed!

10 A key word now appears: "if." The Davidic dynasty will continue *if* (v. 14) David's descendants walk in David's ways, which means: They must worship one God in Jerusalem, 3:10–14.

11 Solomon now puts his "wisdom" into practice—he offers sacrifice in *Jerusalem* (1 Kings 3:15), not *Gibeon*, 1 Kings 3:3,4.

12 Solomon's officials are listed, 4:1–6. He divides his realm into twelve districts, and appoints officials to control these, 4:7–19a. Some equate the Messianic era with Solomon's reign, 4:20, 25.

13 Solomon's borders and needs are described, 4:21–24. Solomon apparently had a large army, which helped control the nation, 4:26,27.

14 More is stated about Solomon's wisdom, 4:29–34.

Solomon Builds the Jerusalem Temple

1 Solomon arranges for the building of the Jerusalem Temple—with Phoenician help, 5:1–12.

2 Although Solomon says David was too busy with military ventures to build the Temple (5:3), 2 Samuel 7:1 says David had "rest" from his enemies. Furthermore, 2 Samuel 7:4–7 states that God did not want a Temple.

3 Solomon makes use of Israelite forced labor in his building projects, 5:13–18.

4 Ch. 6 describes the building, ornamentation, and equipping of the Temple. It takes seven years to build, 6:38.

5 It takes Solomon thirteen more years to complete his other extensive building projects, 7:1–12.

6 Solomon dedicates the Temple, ch. 8. The Ark of the Covenant is placed beneath the wings of the cherubim, 8:6–9. (This narrative was written before the Temple was destroyed in 587 B.C., 8:8.)

7 God bestows divine approval on the Temple, 8:10. (The Holy of Holies had no lighting fixture—it was in darkness, 8:12; note Luke 23:44–46.) The Temple supposedly would stand forever, 8:13.

8 Solomon validates his building of the Temple, 8:14–21. Although he says God had never previously chosen a place "for His name" to dwell, Jeremiah 7:12 insists that Shiloh was the first place God chose!

From Saul to Josiah (continued)

9 Note the "if" in 8:25; the Temple should not be viewed as a permanent structure, 8:22–26.

10 Indeed, only God's "name" dwells in the Temple, while God lives in heaven, 8:27–30. Possibly the final writer was influenced by the destruction of the Temple in 587 B.C., and is pointing out that, although the Jerusalem Temple is gone, God is alive and well in heaven.

11 A number of prayers follow; see 8:31–45. The prayer in 8:46–53 suggests that the people are already in exile. When the people pray, they are always to face the Promised Land, Jerusalem, and the Temple, 8:48.

12 1 Kings 9:1–9 must be read very carefully, and the use of the word "if" in 9:4,6 must be noted. "If" the people worship other gods, they will lose the Davidic dynasty, the land, Jerusalem, the Temple, and their status as God's people.

13 Solomon gives Hiram of Tyre twenty Galilean cities as payment for his building debts, 9:10–14; 2 Chronicles 8:2 edits this information somewhat.

14 More follows about Solomon's building ventures, 9:15–22. The writer now suggests that Solomon used only non-Israelites as slaves, while his own people acted as officials and military personnel.

15 Solomon establishes a port city at Ezion-geber in the Gulf of Aqabah, 9:26–28. This gives the Israelites and Phoenicians trade access to countries to the east. After all, at that time, there was no Suez Canal.

16 The queen of Sheba visits Solomon (ch. 10), and is most impressed by his court—which is described in lavish terms. Tradition says she became pregnant by Solomon (10:13), and her son or grandson became the first king of Ethiopia.

17 An interesting possibility emerges when 1 Kings 10:23–25 is compared with Matthew 2:11; note also Matthew 12:42, 1 Corinthians 1:24. These passages suggest that the visit of the wise men to Jesus had a much bigger meaning than that traditionally assigned to it.

18 Apparently Solomon engaged in the arms trade to fund his building ventures, 10:26–29.

19 Solomon had 700 wives and 300 concubines, 11:1–8. He is not attacked for having them; he is attacked for running after their gods! See 11:4,6, which stresses that Solomon did not walk in the ways of David—he did not worship one God in one place!

20 Solomon is told that his kingdom will split, 11:9–13. The Northern Kingdom will consist of ten tribes, Judah of one (but see 12:21).

21 Edom (11:14–22) and Syria (11:23–25) break away from Solomon's realm and rule.

22 Jeroboam is told that he will become king of the Northern Kingdom, 11:26–37. His dynasty will last forever, if he walks in the ways of David, 11:38. Obviously, he cannot permit his people to continue to worship in Jerusalem—it is in the Southern Kingdom!

23 Solomon tries to have Jeroboam killed, but Jeroboam escapes by fleeing to Egypt, 11:40.

24 Solomon dies, 11:41–43.

The Kingdom Divides

1 Solomon's son, Rehoboam, automatically gains control of Judah, 11:43. However, he fails to gain control over the northern part of the realm, 12:1–24. Had he heeded the advice offered by his elders, he might have done so, 12:6,7.

2 Jeroboam is made king of Israel (12:20) and establishes shrines at Bethel and Dan, 12:25–33. Naturally, he cannot permit his people to worship in a capital city (Jerusalem) controlled by another dynasty, and in a Temple beyond his borders.

3 It is likely that the calves Jeroboam set up in Dan and Bethel were replicas of the cherubim in Solomon's Temple. It is important to note that the prophets do not attack these calves as "idols."

4 The writers of 1 and 2 Kings detest Jeroboam and all northern kings. They walked in the ways of Jeroboam (1 Kings 12:28,29), the son of Nebat, and did not, like David, worship one God in one place—in the Jerusalem Temple.

5 The key to understanding the theology of 1 and 2 Kings is found in 1 Kings 3:1–15; 11:4,6–8. These passages view any shrine other than the Jerusalem Temple as a "high place" or invalid shrine—including those built before the Temple was constructed.

Josiah

1 The first king to take significant steps to centralize worship in Jerusalem was Hezekiah (715–687 B.C.). The reign of Hezekiah is described in 2 Kings 18:1–20:21. Apparently, he carried out some kind of reform movement, 18:1–8; see also 2 Chronicles 29:1–11 (note vv. 5–7); Isaiah 36:7.

2 Hezekiah apparently did not achieve his goal. Possibly any progress he made in this direction was undone by his son Manasseh (687–642 B.C.), whose son Amon ruled for only two years (642–640 B.C.) before being killed by "the people of the land," 2 Kings 21:19–26.

3 The reign of Josiah is outlined in 2 Kings chs. 22,23. In 621 B.C., he centralized all worship in Jerusalem—a state of affairs that became the yardstick by which the worth of all kings of Israel and all previous kings of Judah was evaluated.

4 Josiah was a son of Amon. Although Josiah ruled for 31 years (640–609 B.C.), we are told little about his reign, except for the reform he initiated in 621 B.C., and his death.

5 Josiah's period of rule is given the highest approval rating, 22:2; 23:24,25.

6 During his reign, repairs on the Temple were undertaken, 22:3–7.

7 During the course of these repairs, a "book of the law" was found, and read to Josiah, 22:8–10.

8 Josiah sought an official interpretation of the book's message from Huldah, a prophetess, 22:14–20. She said that, although Judah would soon be destroyed, Josiah would be spared to die in peace. However, Josiah was eventually killed by the Egyptians, 23:28–30.

From Saul to Josiah (continued)

9 The king played a leading role in the ensuing covenant renewal ceremony, 23:1–3. Verse 3 is deserving of careful thought, and what follows throws light on what this piece of Deuteronomic theology means. (See Deuteronomy 10:12,13.)

10 Josiah now began to reform worship life in Judah (23:4–14), and in what was left of the former Northern Kingdom, 23:15–20.

11 He begins by throwing out of the Jerusalem Temple the vessels that had been used for Baal worship and Assyrian astral worship, burning them, and throwing their ashes over the shrine Jeroboam I of Israel had established at Bethel, 23:4. Bethel had been the royal shrine of the Northern Kingdom, Amos 7:10–13.

12 Two groups of priests are referred to in 2 Kings 23:5: "idolatrous priests" and "those also who worshiped the Baals and the Assyrian astral deities." The first group of priests, who were otherwise orthodox, are referred to as *idolatrous* because they officiated at shrines other than the Jerusalem Temple; the issue at stake was geographical location. The second group of priests ("those also") served at shrines that were obviously pagan.

13 Next, Josiah undertakes a thorough cleansing of the Jerusalem Temple and its environs, 23:5–14. He does away with Baal worship, Assyrian astral worship, male prostitutes, the weaving of hangings for Asherah, the horses and chariots dedicated to the worship of the sun, the altars of Ahaz and Manasseh, child sacrifice, and the worship of the gods of neighboring nations (the latter introduced by Solomon).

14 Josiah invites the "idolatrous priests" (referred to in 23:5) to join the staff of the Jerusalem Temple, 23:9. He would not have done so had they been literally idolatrous and pagan.

15 What was wrong with these priests and their shrines was not their *theology*, but their *geography*. *Josiah was now centralizing all worship in the Jerusalem Temple.*

16 After dealing with Judah, Josiah moves into the former Northern Kingdom where he destroys all shrines within its borders, and kills the priests officiating at those shrines, 23:15–20; they were not Levites, 1 Kings 12:31. (It would seem that 1 Kings 13 is a *midrash*, or commentary, on 2 Kings 23:16–18.)

17 Next, Josiah commands the people to hold a Passover observance in Jerusalem, 23:21–23. The text does not say that the people had not been observing the Passover; they had been doing so. The key word in 23:22 is "such." The point is that, from then on (621 B.C.), the people observed the Passover and all other festivals, and offered all sacrifices, in only one place: Jerusalem. This practice is reflected in Joshua 5:10–12, where all Israelites celebrated Passover in one place, Gilgal.

18 Most likely, the book found during Josiah's refurbishing of the Jerusalem Temple (22:8–10) was Deuteronomy. The consensus of opinion is that Deuteronomy was used in the Northern Kingdom to spearhead an attempt, made just prior to 721 B.C., to centralize all worship in that realm—most likely at Shechem or on nearby Mt. Gerizim. The hope was that such a move would stave off the impending march on Israel by the Assyrians. The Northern Kingdom's "repentance" did not prevent the Assyrian advance. Some of the northern priests saw the writing on the wall—and fled south. They took with them some of their sacred writings, including Deuteronomy, and placed them in the store rooms attached to the Jerusalem Temple. In 621 B.C., workmen repairing the Temple found this "book of

the law." Its discovery provided the impetus for Josiah's reform and the centralization of the nation's worship life in Jerusalem.

19 Although Deuteronomy frequently says that the people were to worship their one God in one place, it nowhere attaches a name to that place, Deuteronomy 12:5,11,14,18,21,26; 14:23; 16:2,11. However, in Exodus 20:24 Moses permits the people to worship in many places. As stated in point 18 above, most likely the reference in Deuteronomy is to Shechem or Mt. Gerizim. When the book was found in 621 B.C., those who read it interpreted the term "the place where the Lord made His name to dwell" to refer to the Jerusalem Temple.

20 Whoever wrote or completed 1 and 2 Kings (and possibly Joshua through 2 Kings) in Babylon (2 Kings 25:27–30, 560 B.C.) based his evaluation of the worth of any king from either Israel or Judah on his attitude toward the Jerusalem Temple. This conviction established itself in 621 B.C.—the time of Josiah's reform. Hence, the writer or editor dismisses all northern kings as evil. They walked in the ways of Jeroboam, "the son of Nebat, who caused Israel to sin," 23:15. They, like Jeroboam before them, stopped their people from worshiping in the Jerusalem Temple. Only those southern kings who honored the Jerusalem Temple, and promoted worship within it, could be called "good." Only they walked in the ways of David, who worshiped one God in one city, Jerusalem!

21 There is reason to believe that 2 Kings originally ended at 23:25, and that the writer celebrated the idea that Josiah had restored the Davidic Kingdom. However, despite Josiah's reform, Judah was destroyed by the Babylonians—and, in 23:26–25:30, the writer outlines Judah's last days. The final four verses of ch. 25 contain a message of hope. King Jehoiachin is still alive! Perhaps he will lead the people back to Judah and reestablish the Davidic realm.

22 After the centralization of the sacrificial system in the Temple, provision was made for worshipers from far and near to purchase sacrificial animals inside the Temple precincts. And because only coins bearing no image could be used in making those purchases, money-changers (controlled by the Temple priests) set up shop in the vicinity.

23 Josiah's reform set the stage for the situation Jesus had to deal with when He entered Jerusalem five days prior to His death, Mark 11:1–19; Matthew 21:12,13; Luke 19:45–48. Jesus did not attack the Temple as such. He attacked the corrupt practices taking place within it. Jesus' death was not sought by the ordinary people of the land, but by the religious leaders—for whom the name of the game was power and money! What has changed?

David According to 1 & 2 Chronicles

7

The Temple in 1 and 2 Chronicles

The Chronicler's Goal

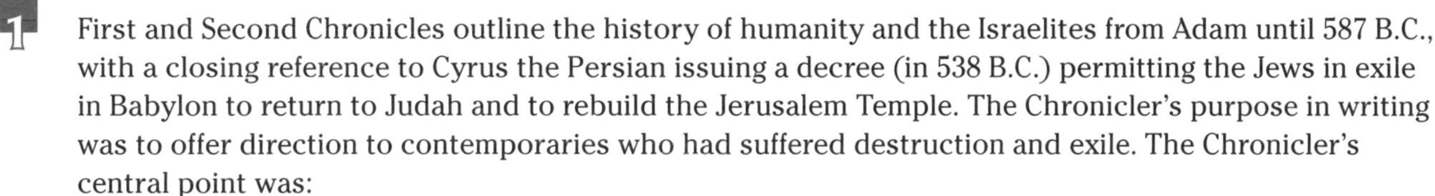

1 First and Second Chronicles outline the history of humanity and the Israelites from Adam until 587 B.C., with a closing reference to Cyrus the Persian issuing a decree (in 538 B.C.) permitting the Jews in exile in Babylon to return to Judah and to rebuild the Jerusalem Temple. The Chronicler's purpose in writing was to offer direction to contemporaries who had suffered destruction and exile. The Chronicler's central point was:

> The Babylonian exile was a catastrophe. It must never be permitted to happen again. How can this be achieved? We, God's chosen people, must strive to be the kind of people God intended us to be.

2 In the first ten chapters of 1 Chronicles, the writer uses *genealogical tables* to cover the period from the beginning of time to Saul, 1:1–9:44. The only information the writer gives about events in Saul's life is, ironically, an account of his death, 1 Chronicles 10. The Chronicler shows considerable interest in the tribe of Judah, 1 Chronicles 2:3–17.

3 Remarkably, 1 Chronicles chs. 1–9 make no reference to:

a. Creation;

b. the patriarchal period;

c. the exodus from Egypt;

d. the events at Sinai;

e. the wilderness wanderings;

f. the conquest under Joshua;

g. the period of the judges.

4 The Chronicler devotes nineteen chapters to the life of David, 1 Chronicles chs. 11–29. He proposes to establish and defend the legitimate claims of the Davidic monarchy in Israel's history, and to underscore the place of Jerusalem and its divinely established Temple worship system as the center of religious life for the Jewish community of his day. If Judaism is to survive and prosper, it will have to heed the lessons of the past, and serve God in the one place where God has chosen to dwell—the Jerusalem Temple. From the Chronicler's point of view, David's reign is the ideal to which all subsequent rulers in Judah must aspire.

The Chronicler's David

1 The Chronicler introduces Saul only to dispose of him, 1 Chronicles 10. Although the description of Saul's suicide follows 1 Samuel 31:1–13 closely, it omits all unpleasant details about the mutilation of the bodies of Saul and his sons, and emphasizes the reasons for Saul's tragic end, 10:13,14. *All of Saul's sons are wiped out at the battle of Gilboa.* Hence, David does not have to dispose of them; see 2 Samuel chs. 9 and 21. In short, Saul is seen merely as an obstacle to David's kingship—as someone to be removed from the stage of history as quickly as possible.

2 The Chronicler's version of David is very different from that contained in 1 Samuel 16:1 through 1 Kings 2:9. It contains no reference to any of David's sins, but focuses on how David established Israel as a nation, captured Jerusalem and established it as the nation's key religious center, and made every preparation for the construction of the Temple that Solomon eventually built. The writer's central

conviction is that the history of Israel (and the world!) took place so that the Jerusalem Temple might be built, and that the community of Israel might worship the God of Israel within its walls. David himself is presented as virtually an "ecclesiastical" monarch.

3 The Chronicler gives the impression that the true beginning of Israel's history did not have to do with the Exodus and Sinai events. It had to do with the rise to power of David—who is the apple of the Chronicler's eye. He deals with the life of David in four time blocks:

a. David is made king of Judah and Israel, 1 Chronicles chs. 11,12.

b. David brings the Ark to Jerusalem, chs. 13–16 (ch. 17 parallels 2 Samuel 7).

c. David expands his realm, chs. 18–20.

d. David prepares for the building of the Temple, chs. 21–29.

4 In Samuel and Kings, David is presented as a political leader, a man whose strengths and weaknesses endeared him to his people as Israel's greatest king ever. The Chronicler, however, shows only a limited interest in David's political genius. This is understandable, for by the time he wrote, Israel had ceased to be a nation. To be sure, the Chronicler did glory in David's military accomplishments and the splendor of his realm (1 Chronicles chs. 18–20), and emphasized also the Nathan oracle, 1 Chronicles 17; see 2 Samuel 7. However, for the Chronicler, David was primarily the one who organized Israel as a worshiping community. It was David who made Jerusalem, the Holy City, his religious capital. It was David who planned the building of the Temple according to God's directions, 1 Chronicles 28:19. It was David who organized the music of the Temple, and assigned the Levites their duties. Although 2 Samuel 6 says that David alone made the decision to bring the Ark of the Covenant into Jerusalem, the Chronicler says the move was sanctioned by all the people, 1 Chronicles 13:1–5.

5 The ecclesiastical robes with which the writer invests David tend to cover the real David. The Chronicler omits all reference to the following:

a. David's troubles with, and flights from, Saul, 1 Samuel chs. 18–26.

b. David's early "Robin Hood"-like career in the wilderness.

c. David's slaughter of the Amalekites, 1 Samuel 27:8–12.

d. David's attempt to obtain the favor of Judah's elders, 1 Samuel 30:26–30.

e. The early wars between Judah and Israel, 2 Samuel 2:12–17; 3:2.

f. Ishbosheth's period of rule in Israel, 2 Samuel 2:8–10.

g. Joab's murder of Abner, 2 Samuel 3:22–30.

h. David's slaughter of Jerusalem's lame and blind, 2 Samuel 5:8.

i. David's harem, 2 Samuel 3:2–5; 5:13–16; 15:16; 20:3.

j. David's adultery with Bathsheba, and his murder of Uriah, 2 Samuel chs. 11,12.

k. Amnon's rape of Tamar, 2 Samuel 13:1–19.

l. Absalom's murder of Amnon, and his flight, return, revolt, and death, 2 Samuel 13:20–18:33.

m. Sheba's revolt, 2 Samuel 20.

n. The murder of Saul's sons and grandsons, 2 Samuel 21.

o. The struggle between Adonijah and Solomon for the throne, 1 Kings ch. 1.

p. David's deathbed instructions to Solomon to kill Joab and Shimei, 1 Kings 2:1–9.

David According to 1 & 2 Chronicles (cont.)

6 The Chronicler declares that, to the very last, David's mind was engrossed with dreams about the future Temple, 1 Chronicles chs. 28,29. The last words the Chronicler attributes to David constitute one of the finest prayers in the Old Testament, 1 Chronicles 29:10–19.

7 It is interesting to note that, according to 2 Samuel 24:24, David bought the real estate on which the Temple would eventually be built for the equivalent of about twenty American dollars. However, according to 1 Chronicles 21:25, David paid the equivalent of 10,000 U.S. dollars for it. Similarly, the Chronicler speaks of about 3,775 tons of gold and 37,750 tons of silver being used in the construction of the Temple, 1 Chronicles 22:14. David himself gave, from his personal fortune, the equivalent of 115 tons of gold and a 265 tons of silver for use in the construction project, 1 Chronicles 29:3,4. The Temple and the ground on which it stood were indeed precious!

The Chronicler's Solomon

1 The Chronicler outlines the reign of Solomon with a similar emphasis. So keen is the writer to praise Solomon's reign that he suggests it was even more glorious than that of David, 1 Chronicles 29:25; but see 2 Kings 18:5, 23:25.

2 The Chronicler does not mention the following:

a. Solomon's struggle for the throne, 1 Chronicles 23:1ff; 28:3ff, 29:1,22.

b. Solomon's use of Israelite slave labor, 2 Chronicles 2:17,18; 8:7–10.

c. Solomon's gift of twenty Galilean cities to Hiram of Tyre; see 2 Chronicles 8:1,2.

d. Solomon's many wives; his son, Rehoboam, has numerous wives, 2 Chronicles 11:21.

e. Solomon's idolatry, 1 Kings 11:1–13; 2 Kings 23:13.

3 Solomon does not permit one of his wives, a daughter of an Egyptian pharaoh, to live in Jerusalem, 2 Chronicles 8:11.

4 In relation to the Temple:

a. 2 Chronicles 3:1 links the Temple site to Mt. Moriah, where Genesis 22:2 says Abraham was to sacrifice Isaac.

b. The Chronicler suggests that the front porch of the Temple was 180 feet high (Hebrew text), and he nearly doubles the height of the freestanding columns near the Temple's entrance, 2 Chronicles 3:3,4,15. Compare these statistics with those in 1 Kings 6.

c. While 1 Kings 6:31 says the Holy of Holies was separated from the Holy Place by doors made of olive wood, the Chronicler says the two areas were separated by a curtain, 2 Chronicles 3:14 (as it was in Herod's Temple, and, most likely, in the postexilic Temple). He also provides Solomon with a platform on which to pray (2 Chronicles 6:13), because in the postexilic period only the priests were permitted to pray before the altar.

The Chronicler and the Kings of Israel

1 2 Chronicles 10–36 deals with the history of the people of God from the time of Solomon's death until the catastrophe of 587 B.C.

David According to 1 & 2 Chronicles (cont.)

2 The writer pays only passing attention to the Northern Kingdom, and mentions its history only when he must do so in order to make sense out of the history of Judah. His conviction is that the Northern Kingdom never really belonged to the people of God. Why? It had cut itself off from the Davidic dynasty (the only legitimate dynasty), and did not encourage worship in the Temple (the only legitimate shrine) at Jerusalem (the only place in which God made God's name to dwell); see 2 Chronicles 6:5,6 and 13:1–12, especially vv. 5,8. Chronicles makes no mention of the destruction of the Northern Kingdom by the Assyrians in 721 B.C.

The Chronicler and Later Kings of Judah

Although the Chronicler idealizes the reigns of David and Solomon, he changes his approach when dealing with Solomon's successors. What he writes about the later kings is influenced by the concept of retribution for neglect of God's will. He sees the fate of each king as related to his religious or irreligious conduct.

In 2 Chronicles, kings are rewarded or punished as follows:

a. Shisack's invasion of Judah is related to Rehoboam's disobedience, 12:2,12.

b. Asa is afflicted with gangrene soon after unwise behavior, 16:7–12.

c. Jehoshaphat's maritime ventures fail because they involve partnership with a northern king, 20:35–37.

d. Uzziah is afflicted with leprosy because of his pride, 26:16–23.

e. It seems inconceivable that God should have permitted a king as wicked as Manasseh to reign for so long; hence, in Chronicles, Manasseh repents, 33:10–13; see 2 Kings 21:10–16.

f. Josiah's death at the hands of Pharaoh Neco is not without cause, 35:20–25; see 2 Kings 23:28–30.

The point is clear: "Do not treat God lightly, for God takes a dim view of disobedience. God treats the nation as God treats its kings. Therefore, be the kind of people you were intended to be!"

The Chronicler's Focus: The Jerusalem Temple

The work of the Chronicler constitutes a history of Israel's worship life centering on Mt. Zion in Jerusalem. Accordingly, despite the account of David's life in 2 Samuel 16–1 Kings 2:9, the Chronicler says David made preparations for the building of the Temple, planned its worship life, and organized the priestly groups who would function within its walls. The Chronicler thus looks beyond David to the Temple, and beyond the Temple to God.

Why does he do this? The way to avoid a repetition of the Babylonian exile is to take the God worshiped in the Jerusalem Temple as seriously as possible. If David took great interest in the Temple, postexilic Israel should emulate David's example!

What does David's example imply for Israel's spiritual life? To begin with, it is essential that Israel be obedient. The Chronicler stresses this central theme through the manner in which he sets forth Israel's history from Solomon until 587 B.C. To illustrate, 2 Chronicles contains 822 verses, of which 480 describe the reigns of four pious kings and 342 the reigns of seventeen other kings. In doing this, the Chronicler frequently uses words such as "laws," "commandment," "statutes," and terms that have to do with reward and punishment.

4 Furthermore, Israel is called to be a church, a worshiping community, a kingdom of priests and a holy nation, Exodus 19:5,6. It is called to be a people whose life is a liturgy and a divine service. Its activities are to center around the Jerusalem Temple where priests, especially Levites, are to have an indispensable place in the conduct of the worship. Even a cursory reading of the Chronicler's record shows his interest in liturgical activities. Festivals and worship services are frequently described, and the people are always ready to participate in them. For example, the people experience such joy in observing Hezekiah's Passover that they decide to observe it a second time the following week, 2 Chronicles 30:23.

5 The Chronicler betrays a particular interest in those people set aside to supervise the worship life of the nation, namely, the priests and Levites. He frequently stresses the importance of their respective roles. They even take part in military ventures. He takes care to distinguish the priests and Levites from the laity, and all earlier references to laymen participating in a religious function, or entering a holy area, are absent. Accordingly, David's sons are not priests, but officials, 2 Samuel 8:18; 1 Chronicles 18:17. Only priests can take part in the coup which dethrones Athaliah—because the event takes place in the Temple, 2 Kings 11:4–20; 2 Chronicles 23.

1 and 2 Chronicles: Miscellaneous Observations

1 In the Chronicler's writings, the focal point in Israel's history shifts from the Exodus to the establishment of the Jerusalem Temple and the inauguration of its worship rituals and practices.

2 The Chronicler manifests an intense dislike for anything related to the Northern Kingdom. It is possible that he adopts this attitude to prove to the Samaritans the legitimacy of the Davidic dynasty and the worship life centered in the Jerusalem Temple. The Samaritans had cut themselves off from Judah and its worship life about the time the Chronicler was writing.

3 The anti-Northern Kingdom polemic is revealed in numerous ways. When King Abijah of Judah goes to war against Jeroboam I, he delivers a speech prior to the battle. In the speech, Abijah declares it a foregone conclusion that the armies of the Northern Kingdom will be defeated—the northerners do not submit to the Davidic dynasty and have established an illegitimate priesthood, 2 Chronicles 13:4–12. Many from the Northern Kingdom flee to the Southern Kingdom when they observe that the Lord is with Asa, king of Judah, 2 Chronicles 15:9.

4 The Chronicler shows a greater interest in the tribe of Benjamin than any other except Judah and Levi. In the postexilic period, much of the former territory of Benjamin was attached to Judah, 1 Chronicles 8:1–40; 9:7–9; Nehemiah 11:7–9.

5 Significant comments are made about the Ark of the Covenant and the Tabernacle. However, they are at different locations: the Ark is in Jerusalem and the Tabernacle is at Gibeon, 1 Chronicles 16:1,37–42; 21:28–22:1. The two come together only when Solomon dedicates the Temple, 2 Chronicles 5:2–7.

6 The Chronicler's use of numbers gives rise to debate. He seems to take delight in exaggerating the size and glory of the Temple, the number of people from all Israel who pledged allegiance to David, and the size of David's army and personal bodyguard. His numbers should not be seen as a problem, but as a preliminary glimpse of the grandeur, splendor, and abundance that will be Israel's when finally the nation enters the Messianic Age—the focus of all its hopes.

7 Although the monarchy was a thing of the past when the Chronicler wrote, his picture of David is designed to encourage the faithful to look for the time when the promise made to David (2 Samuel 7; 1 Chronicles 17) will be revitalized. Indeed, when that time comes, David's Messianic descendant will be as little like the previous kings of Judah as possible. Hence, perhaps his account of David is a statement about the David that should have been, rather than the David that actually was. Perhaps he is giving his readers a glimpse of the ideal Messianic king many believed would one day come. These points are admittedly hypothetical. It may be that his account of David is meant to focus attention solely on the Temple and, above all, on the God of that Temple.

8 A central concern of the Chronicler's account is to show that Israel can secure its future by continuing to worship God according to the pattern set by David. Hence, the Chronicler presents the Judah of his day as a worshiping community that is a direct extension of the worshiping community God established centuries before through David. Its social and religious structures are those that David created at God's command.

9 Israel's hopes, then, did not reside in what a Messiah might be able to accomplish or reveal sometime in the future. Israel could secure its future by carefully honoring the religious institutions and practices revealed by God to David, handed down to Judah's priests, and kept alive by the remnant that survived the exile and returned to Jerusalem.

10 In the light of the above, the Chronicler viewed the exile as little more than an unfortunate interruption in the otherwise unbroken history of Judah as a worshiping community. In the Chronicler's scheme of things, the reestablishment of the monarchy was not as important as the reestablishment of the proper worship of God in Jerusalem. The people who supported and worshiped at the Temple fulfilled all the important tasks of the period of the monarchy.

11 When the Chronicler wrote, not all of Abraham's descendants recognized the Jerusalem Temple as the only legitimate place of worship. A temple dedicated to the worship of God existed also on Mt. Gerizim in Samaria. The destruction of that temple in 128 B.C. by the Jewish Hasmonean king, John Hyrcanus, led to the final break between Jews and Samaritans.

12 The Chronicler does not see fit to mention the temples Jeroboam established at Bethel and Dan. For him, there could be only one Temple—that in Jerusalem. In his estimation, the northerners did not have a valid priesthood, and their worship was useless, 2 Chronicles 13:9.